Emily

TALKING TO YOURSELF
IS NOT CRAZY

CHANGE YOUR INNER DIALOG
TAKE CONTROL OF YOUR LIFE

It's All In Your Head!

Dr. Larry Markson

_Very Best
Larry_

BALBOA
PRESS
A DIVISION OF HAY HOUSE

ISBN: 978-1-4525-4242-3 (sc)
ISBN: 978-1-4525-4244-7 (hc)
ISBN: 978-1-4525-4243-0 (e)

Library of Congress Control Number: 2011961035

Balboa Press books may be ordered through booksellers or by contacting:

Balboa Press
A Division of Hay House
1663 Liberty Drive
Bloomington, IN 47403
www.balboapress.com
1-(877) 407-4847

Because of the dynamic nature of the Internet, any web addresses or
links contained in this book may have changed since publication and
may no longer be valid. The views expressed in this work are solely those
of the author and do not necessarily reflect the views of the publisher,
and the publisher hereby disclaims any responsibility for them.

The author of this book does not dispense medical advice or prescribe the use
of any technique as a form of treatment for physical, emotional, or medical
problems without the advice of a physician, either directly or indirectly. The
intent of the author is only to offer information of a general nature to help
you in your quest for emotional and spiritual well-being. In the event you use
any of the information in this book for yourself, which is your constitutional
right, the author and the publisher assume no responsibility for your actions.

Printed in the United States of America

Balboa Press rev. date: 12/13/2011

This Book Is Dedicated To YOU!

YOU - the patients who filled my offices and had enough confidence and trust in me to keep me in the game. Being your personal family chiropractor for nineteen years was an honor. You waited and watched, giving me the time to mature and the encouragement I needed to grow both as a person and a practitioner.

YOU - the employees of Queens Chiropractic Center, Markson Management Services, The Masters Circle, and The Cabin Experience who unselfishly shared your skills, contributed your unique talents, and had never-ending faith in my concepts and visions. My achievements are far greater than they ever could have been without you.

YOU - the thousands and thousands who, for whatever reason, selected me as your personal or professional coach, sat in my audiences, read the texts, booklets and articles that I authored, listened to my recordings and still came back for more. I am forever indebted to you and I am acutely conscious that without your ongoing support none of this would have happened.

YOU – the readers who have decided to give it a go and invest your valuable time digesting the ideas presented in, "Talking to Yourself Is Not Crazy." Thank you very, very much!

And to **YOU** my family – Huey, my very beautiful, extremely smart, always-in-my-corner and wonderful wife -- Danna and Rick, my incredible children, Robyn and Rob, my daughter-in-law and son-in-law and the best sparkling treasures any Pop-Pop could have wished for, Brielle, Samantha, Pryce, Brady and Ethan, my grandchildren. You hold me up to the light, and when I shine it is because of you.

TABLE OF CONTENTS

FORWARD
MARK VICTOR HANSEN

Co-creator, #1 New York Times best selling series *Chicken Soup for the Soul* ®
Co-author, *Cracking the Millionaire Code*
and *The One Minute Millionaire*
www.markvictorhansen.com

You're about to read a book that is going to change your life. The book is by a man who knows how to talk to himself effectively – and as he says in his title, talking to yourself is NOT crazy.

I have known Dr. Larry Markson for over two decades. I have personally watched him become vastly successful. He has had countless people come to him and ask how they can imitate, emulate, pass and surpass his great success.

He has set up a system on how to talk to yourself, in order to build yourself into a super-star. He founded and built a Chiropractic Practice Management company that helped thousands of doctors reach abundance. He helped them create happy family lives, happy personal lives, happy health and relationship lives.

Now he wants to share that same brilliance with everyone else. I have watched him stand in front of 4,000 to 6,000 people and get them to do his affirmations, aloud and with great enthusiasm. He actually gets them to write goals, and visualize their goals until they come to pass.

I sat with Larry driving from seminar to seminar and meeting to meeting and I was wowed with his stories, many of which are found in this book. He is going to show you how to talk yourself healthy, talk yourself into happy, talk yourself wealthy, talk yourself successful and talk yourself into the future that you desire and you deserve.

Now with the help of the principles, techniques, technologies, and specifics of this book, you are going to start by going from misfortune to absolute fortune. You are going to take whatever parts of your life are tragic and make them into magic. You are going to go from lack of confidence to sublime and ecstatic self-confidence. You're going to score for yourself. You are going to become an exciting human treasure. You are going to be able to make a difference that makes a difference that leaves a lasting and impactful difference.

The world is going to thank Dr. Larry Markson in their prayers for having sourced and served you with his brilliance, wisdom and insight taking you from where you are to wherever you want to be. You're going to enjoy the trip. Happy reading!

FORWARD
BRIAN TRACY

Best Selling Author
International Keynote and Seminar Speaker
www.briantracy.com

It is a pleasure for me to be able to write this Forward for my dear friend, Dr. Larry Markson. I have known and worked with Larry for more than 20 years, and have come to admire and respect him as one of the finest business people and thinkers in America today.

Larry has now embarked on the teaching of one of the most important and life-affecting subjects ever discovered. The work upon which this book is based goes back more than 2,000 years, and actually forms the foundation of many philosophies, religions, and much of modern psychology. It is called "self-talk."

Psychologists have discovered that 95% of your emotions are determined by the way you talk to yourself as you go through your day. Dr. Martin Seligman of the University of Pennsylvania did 25 years of research into human motivation and optimism. He discovered that your "explanatory style" largely determines your reactions and responses to the world around you, and how they affect you.

One of Larry's great insights is that, "That it is not what happens to you, but the way that you interpret what happens to you, that largely determines how you feel and respond."

In "Talking To Yourself Is Not Crazy," Dr. Markson leads you, step-by-step, through an understanding of your "inner dialog," and how you can take complete control of your life, your relationships, your fortune and your destiny by simply taking control of the stream of conversation that flows through your mind, like a river, throughout the day.

Larry has worked with many thousands of people from both tremendously successful and tragic failures. He has seen and experienced the enormous impact that this ongoing, off and on controlled conversation can have in every part of a person's life.

One of the most important insights in this book is Larry's discovery that you can "pre-program" your mind in such a way that external events trigger the kind of internal dialog that enables you to remain calm, happy and effective.

By deciding in advance how you will react to any particular person or event, you can pre-set your almost automatic response mechanism in such a way that you remain in complete control of your thoughts and emotions.

By talking to yourself in a positive way throughout the day, you eventually build a predisposition to be a positive, happy person. Just as athletes engage in regular physical exercise to remain fit and prepared to perform at their best, you can engage in regular "mental exercise" to become the very best person that you can be.

Dr. Larry Markson brings together years of research and experience into a simple, practical, proven system of thought and action that you can apply to immediately improve the quality of your life and relationships, increase your energy, boost your influence and effectiveness in your business, get better results in sales and negotiations, and build a more profitable practice that perhaps you ever imagined possible.

As Larry tells you, the most important part of his teachings is contained in the actions that you take immediately after learning something that you think can be helpful to you.

From this moment forward, as you read these pages, think of how you can immediately apply what you have learned to improve how you think, feel, respond, react and perform in each part of your life. You are in for a wonderful experience!

FORWARD
RICHARD FLINT

Author, TV and Radio Personality
Personal Development Speaker
www.richardflint.com

Some might refer to Dr. Markson's book as brilliant. I would agree. It provides the reader with a simplistic understanding of many of the things that go on inside us. We are all unique, but many don't understand their uniqueness.

Some might refer to "Talking To Yourself Is Not Crazy" as a book everyone one should read. I would agree with their statement. Some books are written to be skimmed. You can read the first lines of each chapter and know everything that is contained in the rest of the pages. Some books are read and as they are being read, the reader is thinking of all the people they know who should *read this book*. Other books are written to be studied. "Talking To Yourself Is Not Crazy" is a book that needs to be studied.

Each chapter is filled with the wisdom necessary to gain insights for a person to learn about themselves from the inside out. In truth this is the only way one can learn who they are and what they need to do to improve from the point where they are in their life.

For me I would say "Talking To Yourself Is Not Crazy" is a book that is needed! What Larry has done in these pages is more than brilliant, more than a book everyone should read; it is a book that moves from page to page offering the reader a glimpse into their own being. With his background and years of gaining insights into the human psyche as a chiropractor, a business creator, a mentor, teacher, an author, a speaker and a person who cares about a person from the inside out, he uses the pages of his book to reach inside the reader, grab them where they *are* and guide them down a pathway that allows them to become who they *can be*.

Most people have the desire to improve, but are lost in a world where sameness has become okay. Most people seek to improve, but find it challenging to find a thought out process that puts the growth puzzle together.

Now, they don't have to search anymore! "Talking To Yourself Is Not Crazy" is what they need! The thoughts he offers, the simplicity of his approach and the challenges he presents are all there for the reader to grasp, understand and implement to achieve a better life.

Well done Dr. Larry Markson! We have needed a work like this and now it is here.

FORWARD
DR. GUY RIEKEMAN

President
Life University
Marietta, Georgia
www.life.edu

I've known Dr. Larry Markson for over three decades and an entire book could and probably should be written on the way he's coached and inspired people from all walks of life to realize their dreams. For them it was life changing, but I believe for Larry it was commonplace; not because he wasn't mindful of the power of realizing someone's highest aspirations, but because he always saw something more in a person than they saw in themselves and lived in the belief that they could find some inner power, some inner resource that once identified could bring forth a path to realization.

There are some images that resonate through my mind when I think of Larry, the transformational words in this book and his life of service.

The first is the concept of BE and DO. When you look at great performers, be they great parents, athletes, chiropractors, etc., they have all come to the realization that what they believe about themselves will become the limit of what they can accomplish and that to accomplish more they must first change who they are - that "Who we "BE" determines what we are capable of doing!"

Larry has taught us that simple yet profound formula; the one that starts off with the recognition that awareness is the first step in the development of high performance. The masters in our environment have produced phenomenal results in life. On the surface these accomplishments seem to be a consequence of hard work, but underneath this enviable commitment to do whatever it takes is a recognition that we get to choose our belief systems – and our belief systems create our success.

The problem is that most of our limiting beliefs are cemented in very early childhood and limit our results as adults. Larry is a master at helping people identify and change these belief systems by teaching you how to talk to yourself until you actually *become someone new*. Without this shift, all change is transient.

The second image I have of Larry is an unstoppable charismatic drive for precision and integrity. Attend one of his seminars and you'll see an environment of calculated perfection that causes you to expect the best out of your own life. And nothing will stop him.

This same drive was always applied to the principle of integrity and I think Larry has always realized what the Dalai Lama said, that if we can live our lives with integrity we can enjoy them twice; once while we live them and at the end when we look back on our lives.

And my final image of Larry is encapsulated in a story he told about coming down the stairs in the middle of the night to get a drink of water. In his pajamas, barely awake he opens up the refrigerator door, the light hits him and he does 30 minutes of lecture! Larry is always "ON" whether at a seminar or in a private consultation or certainly in this book.

So, as I read through this manuscript, I was thrilled to see that my friend of 30 years has shared his most important work of BEING

AND DOING with his usual charming and insatiable drive for precision and integrity in a way that will give you the keys to building the life you have always known is just around the next corner.

Larry will walk you around that corner and this book will become a cherished part of that journey. I hope that all of you get to meet my friend in person at some point. If you do, I can promise he will do 30 minutes of life changing stuff because he is always "ON", but until then read, be and do what he has so masterfully written in this book.

FORWARD
WILLIAM D. ESTEB

Creative Director – Patient Media, Inc.
Author – Patient's Point of View Series
www.patientmedia.com

I met Dr. Larry Markson on a cold Colorado evening in October of 1981 at a chiropractor's office in Colorado Springs. The actor we had hired to play the role of the chiropractor in our Peter Graves implementation video just couldn't get his lines right. Take after take after wasted take. It was getting late. A quick meeting was held. What should we do?

That's when Larry stepped out in front of the camera and literally saved the production. To the crew, this energetic man from New York became known as "One Take Larry." Clearly, the words were in his muscle. In his sinew. In his very soul.

That's the intensity and conviction you are about to see manifested in the pages ahead. My friend Larry has artfully condensed his many years of life experience and coaching wisdom into a convenient and easily accessible format.

On the pages that follow you'll find the pearls, the stories and the principles that one acquires by being fully invested in the game. These lessons come from having the discipline of meticulously attending to details and the ability to make subtle distinctions that many are unable to see or discern. Each chapter is a gold mine for those who want and expect the best from themselves and have the desire to see it in others.

Go slow.

This isn't a novel. Or a self-help book with drills or shortcuts to achievement. Instead, you're about to get a private glimpse inside the mind of one of those rare individuals who has been a student of success principles. He is an accomplished guide among those seeking success in all its many forms. So savor each essay. Mull it over and extract the "success nutrition" from every page. It's here and yours to get.

As it is written in the scriptures:

> "Get wisdom, get understanding;
>> do not forget my words or swerve from them.
> Do not forsake wisdom, and she will protect you;
>> love her and she will watch over you.
> Wisdom is supreme; therefore get wisdom.
>> Though it costs all you have, get understanding.
> Esteem her, and she will exalt you;
>> Embrace her, and she will honor you.
> She will set a garland of grace on your head
>> and present you with a crown of splendor."

Dear reader, you hold in your hands the distilled truth and profound lessons that were learned the hard way, tested, refined and so generously shared here. Chew slowly and deliberately, unpacking the significance and nuance of every story and example.

And then talk it up—to yourself and with others.

PREFACE

Talking To Yourself Is Not Crazy is more than just the title of this book. It is how I, day after day, week after week, and year after year, re-programmed myself to the concepts, visions, attitudes, and belief systems that would ultimately change my life for the better. And they did, only with far greater return than anything I even dared to dream about.

I talk to myself and I am not crazy. I do affirmations daily; I write specific goals and monitor them regularly; I spend hours visualizing (picturing what I want as if it were already mine) and I learned to meditate, to slow down my left brain, and utilize the unlimited power of my right brain, the brain of creation.

I talk to myself when I read some of the things I wrote (much of which is in this book) aloud and with emotion. Later I learned that it is emotion that opens the trap door between the conscious and subconscious minds.

The rest is history for me and for the thousands of people that I have had the privilege of coaching and consulting with over the years. They are not crazy either – but most of them are wiser, happier, far more content and fulfilled and enjoy better lives than before they started *talking to themselves.*

That's right, regardless of what anyone says, Talking To Yourself Is Not Crazy, especially when you do it on purpose, as an instrument to bolster your confidence and strengthen your ability for peak performance.

Self-talk is what you think and say about yourself, *both in your head and aloud*, each and every morning of your life and throughout the day. It is a method of helping you to feel good about yourself, to pepper your subconscious mind with thoughts and emotions that you want to embed, so that when the time comes you can reference and express them with sincerity and conviction.

The self-talk that I am speaking about in this book is the talk you use to either simply program your brain to attract what it is that you want to create in your life or to overcome adversity and turn your thinking process around to something more productive.

You see, whether you like it or not, as long as you are alive, there will be times that you will have to deal with one or more of life's challenges – in fact, you can count on it. Sooner or later something is going to rock your boat and upset your apple cart.

Stuff happens. It is inevitable. And, believe it or not, often times, stuff happens to test your inner strength and to provide you with an opportunity for personal growth.

Of course, the extent to which life's pitfalls and difficulties affects you is determined by your perspective, your past experience, the degree of ownership you take in the problem or situation and your individual personality characteristics.

I want to make it crystal clear that the self-talk you use BEFORE adversity strikes (your daily affirmations, etc.) is more important for preventing problems and negative circumstances than the self-talk you scramble to use AFTER they happen.

How you talk to yourself before you experience any misfortune has everything to do with the way it affects you and how you decide to work through it. Negative self-talk (fear and worry, anxiety-producing statements and feeling sorry for yourself) makes it more difficult to shake off the negatives you are feeling and extends your recovery time indefinitely. Why? Because this kind of self-talk inhibits you from accepting the circumstances you find yourself embroiled in and stops you from being able to move on.

However, when you use self-talk that promotes self-confidence, it becomes easier to maintain a positive perspective. When trouble does strike, you can employ conscious and positive self-talk to lessen its impact, enhance creativity, build optimism, change states and support a healthy self-image.

What a cool tool! "I am getting through this" or "This is just a set-back that I will overcome" or "I will deal with it and move on" or "This calls for the courage I have been storing up" or "This setback (whatever it is) is trying to teach me a lesson that I need and want to learn."

Whatever the words, the important thing is to consciously *Talk to Yourself* using positive, constructive and pro-active statements and by reading narratives such as those appearing on the following pages.

You must first purge your brain from its past habitual repetitions and then input the program and thinking patterns that you want it to use to attract your newfound health, happiness, success, and fulfillment.

Start talking to yourself RIGHT NOW! Pepper your mind with the thoughts you want to embed. Say your daily affirmations out loud and with enthusiasm, remembering it is emotion that opens the door from your conscious mind to your subconscious mind. Do this again and again and again. Repeat and Review with

Regularity (RRR) everything you want to be or become, until what you say or think sticks.

Mentally talk to yourself (repeating thoughts, actions and feelings) and tell yourself who you are and want you want, NOT what you don't want!

Finally, I would ask you to realize that *Talking To Yourself Is Not Crazy*. It is, in fact, the one of the most significant tools you can use to transform your entire life!

INTRODUCTION

It is no exaggeration if I start off by stating, with absolute certainty, that a strong positive self-image is the best possible preparation for success in your career, as well as in your life.

Most psychologists identify low self-esteem as the root cause of failure and mediocrity, and I agree. My knowledge comes from years of observing a myriad of people – watching how they function and how their triumphs or humiliations are absolutely caused by the mental images they have of themselves.

I can promise you that your self-image (the way you see yourself) is the very core of your personality and it determines more about you than any other single factor affecting your business or practice or your personal life. In my study of success over all these years, it became essential for me to understand why self-esteem was so crucial, not only for my personal career, but so I can help all of you become more personally and professionally successful.

As I began to really see how the picture I had of me affected my whole life, I decided right then to reprogram and change that picture for the better, no matter how long it would take…and I strongly suggest you do the same.

Why is the mental picture you have of yourself so crucial a factor in determining how far you will go in your life or your career?

It's because your self-esteem shapes the choices you make – your choice of friends, whether you are entrepreneurial or not, your choice of careers, who you marry, where you choose to live – and how you react to *everything* that happens to you.

It determines your attitude toward yourself and the people around you. Your capacity to grow and learn, the action steps you are willing to take, the appearance of your office, the people you select to hang with, the amount of money you make and even the amount of money you keep – all are affected by your mental self-image.

The way you see yourself has a profound impact on your family relationships, your business relationships and your personal relationships and I have no doubt that those of you who enjoy the most successful business life and home life have the most confidence and the best self-images.

Opening Your Mind So You Can Have It Your Way

WHAT HAPPENED TO ME?

That's probably a good question in a book of this nature, but I choose to spare you the details of being raised in a dysfunctional family. Suffice it to say that there was no award given for parenting skills and my environment matched their low self-esteem. I was unknowingly programmed by a constant barrage of limited thoughts and aberrant behaviors.

Let's just say that the things I learned growing up were the antithesis of the concepts of happiness, success, and fulfillment that are the very purpose of this book. Besides, I just don't want to bore you to death by recounting my so-called rags to riches, Horatio Alger story.

Fast forward to age twenty-nine. I was married and had two children who actually expected me to provide for them, to earn enough money for food, clothing, and shelter. I was a licensed Doctor of Chiropractic, but not doing well in practice (remember my programming) and therefore I had to work several jobs just to keep my head above water.

Finally, my best buddy in the world, Dr. Steve Himmelstein, forced me to attend a "Parker Seminar for Professional Success" with him. By forcing me I mean he volunteered to pay for me, so how could I resist – what did I have to lose? I will admit though that I went kicking and screaming. After all I thought I knew it all, until I discovered that I was scared to death and not really open to anything but what I already believed.

There, at that very seminar, I learned about the *Power of Thought* as an instrument for success and failure and I came to realize that my failure was basically the result of failure thinking. And then I learned that the right use of my mind could become the key to healthy, happy, prosperous, and successful living.

That was it! That was the beginning. That was the awakening and when I realized that while my upbringing was a huge factor in my life, I could now choose to *break free* and *choose my own thoughts and actions*. More importantly, I decided that from then on I would be responsible for my own life, my own happiness, and my own prosperity. And, it all happened in one weekend.

A few years later, the Parker Foundation named me Chiropractor of the Year, probably because I went on to build one of the largest and most successful practices around. Yes, me! And I did it in the same location, in the same small office with the same two assistants working for me (the ones I had been blaming all those years for the cause of my practice failure).

Then a freak accident occurred (or was it a fortuitous event?) that changed my entire life. I tripped on my own two feet walking onto a tennis court and broke my elbow in more places than I could count. End of one career, and fortunately the beginning of another.

I had, after all, learned the thoughts, actions and feelings that could and would allow me to be successful anywhere. This was the opportunity to find out what I was made of.

Since then, I have founded two highly successful personal and professional seminar and consulting businesses (Markson

Management Services & The Masters Circle) and more recently my new and more intimate in size (twenty-five people at a time) Breaking Free – Personal Freedom retreats called The Cabin Experience. All of these businesses were and are based upon the principles, concepts, and thoughts contained in this simple, and in my opinion, powerful book.

TWELVE GEMSTONES THAT CAN CHANGE YOUR LIFE

The following are the Twelve Gemstone phrases or mental keys that actually helped me to change my life and move from failure toward success – *and they can do the same for you.*

These gemstones were the foundational cornerstones upon which I built a new me. They represented my new way of thinking, the concepts, and philosophies I adopted and used as mental anchors. I repeated them to myself over and over again and reflected upon their meaning until this group of mantras started to keep me focused on what I chose to believe.

The dozen gemstones, as I called them, helped me change my mind, alter my thinking, expand my visions and concepts, and gain a greater understanding of what success was really all about.

I implore you to read them over and over again until you truly understand what each one really means. Better yet, make them a part of who you are. The 12 Gemstones are:

1. It's All In Your Head

"It's All In Your Head" is an expression I coined way back in 1980 and to this day it has become the expression that I am linked to and the title of the platform talks I use to open my guest speaking appearances.

These five words, although seemingly simple, deliver the message that the secrets to a deeper spiritual connection, better health, more happiness, personal fulfillment, financial abundance, and long-lasting relationships are found in the six inches between your ears.

The way you have been programmed, the way you think, and the feelings you have, all control the way your behavior patterns cause you to act.

"It's All In Your Head" refers to your self-image and self-esteem – the BE portion of Be, Do and Have. That self-image causes the way you walk, the manner in which you talk, the words you select, the cadence of your sentences, the people you attract or repel in and out of your life, the colors you wear, the books you read, the things you like or dislike, etc.

All the things in your head that tell you "who you are" and indeed create your success and happiness or the mediocrity and frustration that many erroneously believe comes from their outer world. But it doesn't! It all comes from the inner world – inside your head.

In that cranial vault resides your personal list of securities and insecurities, likes and dislikes, fears and faiths, cans and can'ts, wills and won'ts, plus the guilt, worries, blames, angers and fears that you have allowed to become part of your make-up.

"It's All In Your Head" is an expression that says that "who you are" is the sum total of all your life's experiences and how you have interpreted them. It considers all of your successes and failures, your triumphs and humiliations, the goods, the greats, the bad and the ugly. All of them and how they have, over time, molded not only how you think and act to the situations and issues of your life, but more importantly, how you RE-ACT to them.

Ah, yes. "It's All In Your Head." Now, all you need to do is shed the old, erroneous, and probably useless thoughts, ideas, concepts, and visions from the past and re-program them to more positive and productive ones – and the rest will take care of itself – naturally and with effortless ease.

No one said that this is an easy task to accomplish, for surely that is not true. It takes time (more than many are willing to invest) and effort and determination and guts, but it is worth it. Just ask me -- and the thousands who have found success, happiness, and fulfillment by reprogramming their minds. After all, "It Is All In Your Head."

2. MFTP (Mother, Father, Teacher, Preacher)

You are a potpourri of all your past inputs, whether they were delivered and received by you intentionally and on purpose or inadvertently and subtly without specific intent.

Your parents, your schooling, your peers, your religious training, the mass media, the movies you watch, what you read, what you see, hear, smell, taste and touch, and all of your previous experiences gave you input as to who you are, what you should believe, what you should strive for and what your chances of succeeding were.

It has all been drummed into your poor little head since you were born and, while much of your "pre-programming" is good, some of it is detrimental to your success, health, and happiness in life. In fact, much of what you believe to be true and therefore act upon as if it were true and beneficial for you, is not true at all. It was someone else's "truths" taught to you to keep you safe and out of harm's way.

Obviously, all of the above is a mouthful, and so we have coined an acronym that says it all in four simple letters – MFTP, meaning our Mothers, Fathers, Teachers, and Preachers.

The "M" for Mother stands for the most important influence in all of our lives. The matriarchal influence set the basic framework for your self-image from the moment you were born. The love-giver, the care-taker and nurturer, but also the one who attempted to protect you and keep you safe – the one from whom you learned your lessons of guilt, fear, worry, blame and anxiety.

The "F" for Father stands for the somewhat old-fashioned disciplinarian, the macho strength, and masculine influence. Dear old dad, traditionally and incorrectly labeled as the head of the family, the breadwinner and possibly even a kind and gentle soul, but also a very visible influence on a child's life.

Most of you, by life's circumstances or plain old intuition have gravitated to and favor the teachings and "being" of one or the other – Mother or Father. They are, after all the two major influences in life, the ones who programmed you through all of your formative learning years.

The "T" for Teacher stands for anyone or anything that has ever taught you anything that you believe to be true. The "T" references much more than just your professional teachers. It refers to what you see and read, your experiences and interpretations, the lessons you have learned from living, from history, from observation. Whatever someone or something taught you is the "T" and that "T" has influenced much of the formation of your personality and who you are.

And, finally the "P" for Preacher – used in this context to mean much more that the inputs from clergy. The "P" refers to anyone who has, over time, repeated something to you enough times and with enough conviction and authority to have gained a piece of your mind. The constant and reinforced programming that wore away your defenses until you were responding "as you were trained to respond."

We were TAUGHT and we ACCEPTED from our Mothers, Fathers, Teachers and Preachers some limited thinking which has caused many of us to grow up believing and doing things the same old way. Then we wonder why we get the same old results.

3. Circle – Circle

The term Circle – Circle and indeed a diagram of two adjacent circles standing side by side is the metaphorical geometric symbol that I use to signify a person's Intent (left circle) and, after action, the Experience they receive (right circle).

I selected a Circle for this metaphor because it is complete, smooth, and perfectly symmetrical. There is no beginning or end to a circle. It is, in fact, a great visual model of birth and death, dawn and dusk, cause and effect, ashes to ashes and dust to dust. It is perfect!

With this diagram in mind pretend that the left circle means that someone has "Right Intent." Right Intent is a basic ingredient of all success, health, and happiness. It is when you show up big, meaning you have a higher purpose, a deep conviction, a unique concept and vision, the right attitude, the right plan and you have honesty, ethics and integrity. Then you have Right Intent and the first Circle is complete.

The Circle on the right simply represents the Experience you will receive when you utilize one of the two catalysts that connects the Circles together.

Symbolically, the catalysts reside in the space between the two Circles. The first is signified by a capital "T" and it refers to Telling the Truth. Telling the Truth, as opposed to telling a lie, means showing up the best way you know how to BE – recognizing that you are God's greatest miracle and that there never was, there is no one now and there will never be another just like you. You are one of a kind, with separate fingerprints and a unique identity. You are a miracle and you are supposed to be in charge of your own life.

If the Circle of Right Intent is intact with all of its components and you tell the Truth, based on the Law of Cause and Effect, your "Experience" (symbolized by the second Circle) must match the Circle of your Intent. Circle – Circle. One Circle matches the other. Success!

But, on the other hand, if you have Right Intent (first Circle) and your action is an "L," a Lie (not a lie as opposed to the truth, but rather the meaning we would apply if you do not show up as the best you could be – you are lazy, sloppy, disorganized and procrastination is your friend. You cut corners, do not give your best effort, and think that good enough is good enough).

As a result your Experience is not symbolized by the Circle of Right Intent matching a Circle of what you would Experience. The second diagram now transforms to a "Triangle." You therefore end up with the symbolization of Circle – Triangle.

Circles and Triangles do NOT match geometrically – or in life. So, Circle – Circle equals success and Circle – Triangle equals failure. This explains why you can have right intent and if you have wrong personal action and behavior you will still fail.

I choose Circle –Circle!

4. What's So

The expression, "What's So" means that you are taking *total responsibility* for your own life and that you have decided to live in your CAUSE and not others' effects. You have chosen to re-program yourself to the pleasure of the future and away from the pain of the past.

"What's So" means I see what IS, the intellectual truth of the matter. It says, I see what is, not what I wished were true or what I think was, not what I hoped was – or dreamed was, not what coulda, shoulda, woulda, oughta be, not if only I'da, but what actually is – "What's So!"

What is – IS! Good for me or bad for me. It doesn't mean I take the blame or the fault or the credit or the reward. It does mean that with regard to personal enlightenment there are no rights and no wrongs, just "What's So."

In this philosophy you must take responsibility and choose to live in your cause, not other's effects. You choose to make a new successful mental tape for yourself. You choose not to allow anyone to have dominion over you and you accept total responsibility for your own success.

5. Stuck in Your Stuff

"Stuck in Your Stuff" is a metaphorical saying meaning, fixed in a negative habit pattern in which you accept only what you already believe and already agree. And, because you have accepted this as part of your make-up, you unconditionally reject anything else, such as new concepts, new visions, and more expanded thinking.

Being "stuck" is, at best, survival living because it never allows you to change, even for the better. It comes from needing to be right and needing to win and forces you to run your stuff (tell your story) to yourself and others.

Being "stuck in your stuff" comes from MFTP (Mother, Father, Teacher, Preacher) pre-programming. "They" taught you limited thinking and now without realizing it you believe that your life and the things that happen to you are shaped by circumstance, by external forces, and you become an *outer-directed person!*

Eighty percent of people are "Stuck in Their Stuff" and never attain the happiness they really want, because they HAVE TO DO IT THEIR WAY, which isn't even their way. It is the way of their uninformed "teachers" from the past – MFTPs.

Twenty percent of people seem to have a magic wand, a Midas touch that seems to attract just what they need for success. We think they have an insurance policy against failure, but that's not true! The actual truth is that the successful minority are *inner-directed people* that have simply learned that *they are* the CAUSE and the circumstances in their lives are the EFFECT.

Your "stuff" is planted in your head by others, and you choose to believe them. Your stuff is the stuff in your head – the negative habit patterns and negative feelings, everything in your head that keeps you mediocre and average.

This book will unshackle you from your thoughts of lack and limitation and help you get rid of your "stuff."

6. Passage of Pain

The "Passage of Pain" is the real or perceived difficulty that a person experiences when attempting to transform themselves from one dimension of behavior to another, from their old way of thinking and feeling to another, and from old "Stuck in Your Stuff" negative habit patterns, to new, fresher, freer and more positive ones.

The "Passage of Pain" is the tunnel that you must go through on your journey from "where you are now" to "where you want to be." You must admit that at times it may seem difficult for you to change, especially if you hold on to "being right" or to the fears that shackle you and stop your growth. It becomes easier when you truly understand that the happiness, satisfaction, joy and fulfillment you seek is not to be found in your outside world, but only in the inner attitudes and beliefs that you must change and make your own.

It is a "Passage of Pain" because the development of new habits of thought requires abandoning old ones and that tends to activate your hidden fears – of the unknown that lies ahead, of making a mistake, of failing, of being wrong.

The trip through the unfamiliar (the passage of pain) is well worth the effort and any temporary emotional upset you must face. After all, on the other side of the tunnel are peace, happiness, and security.

7. My Fee Is My Fee, Is My Fee!

The expression, "My fee is my fee, is my fee" requires some explanation because it means that my fee for a particular service or product is fifty dollars non-negotiable, take it or leave it, end of story. It also refers to the inherent value of what you are selling and that does not change and is not raised of lowered based upon what the traffic will bear.

It is not fifty dollars for you -- and forty dollars for someone else. Or, if you appear to be rich, it is sixty dollars for you, and if you say you can't afford it, I'll lower the fee to thirty-five dollars for you.

"My fee is my fee, is my fee" is not a shell game. It has to do with honesty and integrity and the value you set on your service or product and should not whimsically vary from one person to another. Of course, you must factor in the knowledge and expertise you have, the cost to deliver the service or product and the fairness and equitability in the marketplace.

"My fee is my fee, is my fee" says that the price tag you wear on your own sleeve speaks volumes as to the level of your confidence and how you really feel about yourself. I believe that you should not even consider lowering your fees simply to seduce someone to do business with you. Instead, I suggest you work on increasing the perceived value of the service or product and hold your ground until you begin to attract the customer, client, or patient willing to pay your usual and customary fee for that particular service -- plus the outstanding intangible values you provide.

The correct consideration is a fair fee for an outstanding service, and when you do raise your prices or fees, they are only raised when the value and benefits to another increases. In that case, it would be natural that your remuneration escalates to meet that value.

8. Success Comes From You, Not To You!

"Success comes from you, not to you" implies that you are responsible for all that you create or fail to create and that all the ingredients of success are inside you. You were born with them. Some of these ingredients include your concepts, visions, ideas, beliefs, attitudes, energies and the Law of Attraction that resides within and attracts into your life all the people, places, circumstances or events that align with your thinking and feelings.

"Success comes from you, not to you" gives credence to the omnipotent Law of the Universe that says that for every action there is an equal and opposite reaction. That is the Law of Cause and Effect.

This expression says that you emanate (from deep inside you) the vibrations that attract everything you think or feel to yourself as a magnet attracts steel. Therefore, it can be accurately said that success (or failure) comes from you, not to you.

9. If You Are Not Early, You Are Late!

Since punctuality is a tenet of success and procrastination is a characteristic of a poor self-image and failure, and since it is almost impossible to be exactly on time, it stands to reason that it is far better to be early than late.

The expression, "The early bird catches the worm," means that if you are on time or late, everything left over will be diminished or gone – but if you are early, everything will be fresh and plentiful.

Habitual lateness or tardiness comes from a person who, upon inspection, will exhibit several characteristics of a poor self-esteem. These include indecisiveness, the inability to confront people or handle situations that arise, procrastination, disorganization, working or living in a cluttered environment, feeling overwhelmed, and frustration.

10. There Is No Such Thing As a Try!

Simply said, "There is no such thing as a try," means that you are either in the active process of doing something or you are not. For example, if I ask you to "try" to take a hat off my head, you would most likely reach up, perhaps tentatively, but nevertheless you would actually take if off my head. My response, no doubt, would be an apology for being unclear with my instructions. I would then repeat louder, slower and with more enunciation that I wanted you to "try' to take it off my head, but you actually took it off my head.

I would then give you another opportunity to do it again – "try to take it off my head." After actually doing this exercise from the speaker's platform with seminar audiences for many years, the results were clear. Every person asked timidly reached up, took hold of the hat in their fingertips and actually squinted in a mild facial contortion, but *did not* remove the hat from my head.

Either you take the hat off or you don't! Either you are dieting or you are not. Either you have completely stopped drinking or gambling or you have not.

When someone says that they are *trying* to do something, it might mean that they are thinking about it or pondering the available choices, but they are not actively engaged in the action process of "doing it."

The lesson is that you are either doing it or not and there is *no such thing as a try.*

11. Good Enough Is Not Good Enough!

Good enough is NEVER good enough for someone that is fully engaged in the process of self-discovery or personal growth.

"Good enough" is a phrase of mediocrity. It means, "I know it could be better, but it's not worth my effort of time – and I can get by or get away with what I've done. Ugh, perish the thought. No one just "gets by!" It is either butter or margarine. You cannot fool the universe!

It is either done with all your effort, talent, skill, caring and expertise or it is less than that. Beyond good lies the huge arena of great, wonderful, excellent, fabulous, stupendous, incredible, and fantastic!

"Good enough" is for average people who are satisfied with average lives and achievements, but the very concept of "only good enough" is a thorn in the sides of all want to grow to greatness.

12. Belief Is the Master - We Are The Slaves!

If we could summarize into one word the entire essence of most success programs, that word would be "belief." The purpose of the success-striving mechanism within you is to achieve that which you BELIEVE to be true. That is the way our brain functions, like it or not, believe it or not. "Belief is the Master – We are the Slaves!"

It has been said that whether you believe you can or believe you can't, you will probably be right! And, the exciting thing about programming yourself in the area of belief is that you can program and condition yourself to believe ANYTHING YOU WANT.

Just imagine how you would feel if you would re-train yourself and could actually and automatically think thoughts such as, "Yes I can. I am able to do whatever I want to do. I am FREE!"

Developing a new belief system can happen and can happen at any age, but I promise you it takes diligence and total attention. It cannot be left to chance because the outside environment is continually trying to break your bubble and keep you in your place.

Remember that your self-image was formed in your childhood and it won't go away until YOU make it go away.

Whatever you believe to be true (regardless of where that belief came from), you will act on as if it were true – whether the consequences are good for you or bad for you.

Perhaps you do not understand the laws of physics that explain and govern gravity. Or even worse, perhaps you have some inkling of them, but you do not believe them to be true. Perhaps then you would walk to the end of a building and just step off. And, as a result, understand it or not, like it or not, believe it or not, you would find yourself going down.

Your past programming determines many of your beliefs and your beliefs determine who you are, who you aren't, what you will do and what you won't do. You are a slave to your beliefs. The lesson here is to carefully examine all beliefs and work on changing or eliminating any that are limiting or restrictive in nature.

Change your beliefs and you will change your thinking. Change your thinking and you will change your feelings. Change your feelings and you change what you attract into your life.

THE COOKIE THIEF

Oddly enough, I remember the exact date, but not the exact year. I had the honor of sharing the speaker's platform in Toronto with one of my heroes, the one and only Wayne Dyer. Wayne Dyer is a superstar television personality, an international best-selling author, and a fantastic speaker who travels the world enlightening the masses. This was a thrilling moment for me.

He was to speak that evening and I was to follow the next morning and, therefore, I had the opportunity to sit in the audience to listen to him in person.

During his mesmerizing talk, he took a few minutes to read a poem written by a woman named Valerie Cox, whom I had never heard of before. After hearing the poem, I was surer than ever before that what I thought was true, was indeed true. Belief is indeed the master and we are the slaves, just as I described to you in the previous chapter.

I asked Wayne if he would share that poem with me, which he graciously did. The message is so profound that I have often times recounted the story of the poem to my own audiences and want to share it with you now.

The original poem is called "The Cookie Thief" and it was written by a woman named Valerie Cox. (The actual poem can be found in poem form on the internet. I am telling the story of the poem because I have not been granted permission to include it in this book.)

The Story of a Cookie Thief

The poem tells the story of a woman who was waiting at an airport for her plane, but had plenty of time until departure. She ended up in an airport shop, purchased an interesting book and a bag of cookies, then found an empty seat and sat down for the wait before boarding.

Shortly, she put her cookies down on the adjacent seat and became engrossed in her book. It didn't take long for her to become aware of the fact that the man beside her kept grabbing a cookie or two from the bag in between them.

She munched some cookies too while watching the man diminish her stock. The thought of this thief stealing her cookies began to irritate her. When only one cookie was left, the man picked it up and broke it in half. Boldly, he ate one half and offered her the other.

Obviously upset she was relieved when her flight was called and she gathered her things heading for the gate. Upon settling down in her seat she started to rummage through her carry on looking for the book. It was then that she gasped with surprise. There was 'her" bag of cookies in front of her eyes.

It didn't take her long to understand that she had made a terrible mistake and the man was not stealing her cookies but actually trying to share "his" bag of cookies with her!

Too late to apologize she realized with grief, that she was the rude one, the ingrate, the thief.

Great, huh? Did you get the message? The woman at the airport actually believed that the other man was stealing her cookies. After all she saw it, so she believed it to be true. But she was wrong, oh, so very wrong. Yet, her facial expressions and the rest of her physiology were probably now tuned to her belief – perhaps some anger, definitely some resentment. Maybe she had some adrenaline pumping into her system or her blood pressure was elevated.

Who knows, but whatever the case, she believed it to be true and acted upon that perceived truth, yet all along it was false.

Are you a cookie thief or will you choose to shed some of the old beliefs that you have picked up along the way, the ones that were never true in the first place? And, what do you think would happen if you really did so? Yes, you are correct – your world would change for the better!

Thank you, Valerie!

IT'S THE WHO, NOT THE DO

No matter where I go, the number one question I hear everyday, is, "Larry, what can I DO to build a bigger, better and more successful business or practice?" And, believe it or not, it is a question that not only comes from the mouths of new or struggling small business owners or entrepreneurs, but surprisingly enough, from those who have solid medium-level operations and even from those who are the so-called superstars.

"Tell me what to DO" has become the mantra of this generation. Tell me what to DO to get more new business! Tell me what to DO to get people to comply and stay with me longer? Tell me what to DO to stop my employees from turning over so fast... and on and on it goes – DO, DO, DO.

All of you who are in business for yourselves really want to grow more fulfilling and outstandingly successful businesses. Unfortunately, the way you are currently "doing it" isn't working or, according to what I hear, you have been there and done that and nothing seems to be working. Believe me I know the feeling.

I failed big time before I learned to succeed. When I first started to practice way back when, I failed miserably for the first seven years, and it didn't matter that I was raised in a family that utilized the services of a chiropractor and that I loved my profession with all my heart. It didn't even matter that I thought myself to be clinically competent, having graduated at the top of my class.

What did count was that no matter how hard I tried and regardless of all the things that others told me to DO, success in any form was an elusive commodity. In my case, things started to change radically when I started to change *me as a person* and that, of course, changed me as a professional practitioner. Then, and only then, did all the DOs start to be effective.

I decided to change who I was. Yes, although very painful, once I discovered that I was responsible for my own success or failure (Oh no, please say that ain't so!) and that it wasn't the school I graduated from, or my community, or the insurance companies or the competition, etc., I actually made a decision to diligently work on me – *on who I was inside.* Believe me, it wasn't easy to accept that me, myself and I, was causing my failure and not necessarily what I was DOING.

It was my concepts and visions, my beliefs, my securities and insecurities, my lack of confidence, my fear of rejection, my inability to confront, the words I selected, my methods of expression, the limited thinking of the people I hung around with and all the other intangible personality traits that actually caused the lack of results I was experiencing.

An Analogy

Three different vendors, all selling the same service, are invited to do a Health Fair, on the same day, under the same weather conditions and at booths with similar great locations just feet away from each other. The booths are mirror images of one another and so are the vendors themselves – they were all asked to wear blue blazers with tan pants and white shirts.

Each had a similar goal – to attract as many people as possible to their booth, engage them in conversation and explain the amazing health benefits achieved by utilizing their services, and ultimately to get them to make an appointment to go to their offices for a more complete and thorough presentation.

One vendor signed up 25 potential new people, but only 10 showed up and 6 enrolled in the program. Another signed up only 12 new potentials. However, 10 came in and 6 enrolled (the same number as the first one who signed up 25). Vendor number three only made appointments with 7 people, but every one of them came, enrolled in the series and became great enthusiasts of natural health care services and products.

So what was the difference between them? Why do different people DOING the same thing get different results? For the same reason that if I start ten new professional clients at the same time – all graduates from the same college, all 32 years old (tall, thin and extremely handsome or beautiful), all practicing within a one-mile radius of one another, all using the same techniques and all using the same strategies and action steps to succeed – one year later they would have ten different success results.

How could that be? They sit in the same seminars, listen to the same lectures, read our text, listen to the same CDs and do the same affirmations, etc. It is because of WHO they are inside the skin and not necessarily because of what they DO.

You see it is WHO you are, not only what you DO that determines your success in business and in life. It is a person's identity that determines how effective the action steps taken will turn out. It is a combination of a person's purpose, their energy and enthusiasm, their belief in what they do, their desire to make a difference in a patient's health and how they communicate their message that makes all the difference in the world. Remember, people won't ever *buy* the message, without first *buying* the messenger – their concept of who they are and what they stand for.

Success is, in fact, very personal. It is about your clarity, your congruency, your determination, your guts, and audacity to be different and to stand for a higher purpose while aligning with all the great principles of success.

And clearly, I am not saying that you shouldn't know what to DO! You must indeed become an expert in all the strategies, procedures, protocols, and action steps that build and operate your particular business. Yet, be forewarned that regardless of the skills you have acquired, when push comes to shove, "It's the WHO, not the DO."

You are hereby notified that success, health, and happiness are part of your destiny and you can claim them anytime you wish. This is not an idle statement or some trivial positive jargon from a personal and practice development coach. And it is not meant to encourage you beyond your capabilities. It is the truth of *who you are.*

STRATEGY-BASED VS. IDENTITY-BASED

The distinguishing feature that separates my philosophy of success with others is that it is uniquely "Identity-based," and not merely "Strategy-based," similar to the Who vs. the Do of the previous chapter.

"Strategy-based" means that you are told what action steps need to be taken for you to get quicker and better results, such as holding team meetings regularly, enforcing your principles, policies and procedures, customer or patient education, methods of client retention, proper fees, payment options and collections, overhead containment, better efficiency, staff training, public speaking and running the business more effectively. Simply, it means telling you what to DO and, based on what you DO, you will get what you want.

Oh, if that were only true, life, business, and success would be so very easy. We'd tell you what to do, when to do it, how to do it and why to do it that way…and poof, as if by magic, everyone taught a given procedure would reach the same outstanding level of achievement.

Sadly though, just telling you what to DO (a strategy to act upon) does not get the results the teacher wants. For example, if I taught different people the same exact method of conducting a highly successful "bring in more business technique," and those now thoroughly-trained individuals took the same identical action steps, they would get different results, some outstanding and some outstandingly poor.

Why? Because different individuals with different IQs, different levels of skill, different belief systems, different levels of confidence and security, and different abilities to confront and face rejection *always* get different results. Pure logic would say that they all possessed different knowledge, communication skills, attitudes, desires, abilities to bounce back from adversity and a whole host of other contributing factors.

Hence, strategy-based advice by itself is limited and works for some better than others. When it does work it is not because of the strategy, it is because of the person who is applying that strategy and most importantly, the *identity* of that individual.

Identity means, "Who you are determines how well what you do works." It means who you are way down deep inside, your desires, your likes or dislikes, your confidence or fears, your willingness to adapt and change or even your "I'm just fine the way I am" attitude. Basically, I'm talking about your self-image, your self-esteem, your values hierarchy and the behavior patterns that define everything you do or do not do, and even how well you do them.

Achievement then is always based on who you are! So, what seems to be the problem here? Why do people enthusiastically join a Personal, Business or Practice Development Program with the unreasonable expectation that within a short period of time they will be able to change their complete identity, eliminate their past and pre-programming, and become an entirely different person?

While that does happen for a select few, changing yourself into a successful person who then builds a successful business or practice is *a process that requires considerable time*, perhaps even years. This sounds a lot like what doctors tell their patients about healing, doesn't it?

So, given the time, what then is the ingredient that is required?

Courage is the answer.

I know that sounds too easy, too simple, and you want me to conjure up some far more exotic and complex ingredient. But I assure you there is none. All that is required is *courage* and the burning desire to change. It has never been a question of *can* you change…of course you can! It has always been a question of *will* you change. Well, will you?

Do you have the courage, the guts, the audacity, the tenacity and the determination to shed old habit patterns regardless of how uncomfortable that might be, and persist until new, healthier and more successful habit patterns replace them? That calls for making a major decision. And, by the way, *courage is a decision,* and no one can give it to you. It cannot be purchased or earned by being nice or by doing good deeds. Courage is already within you! Perhaps it is dormant, but it is there. *Courage comes from you, not to you!*

Defined, courage is the state or quality of mind or spirit that enables one to face danger, fear, or vicissitudes with self-possession and bravery. People don't change because they are afraid to change, although after years of trying and failing, their minds now tell them that they are okay just the way they are.

Just remember that change takes time and hard work. It is not for the faint of heart, the procrastinators, or the lazy. It requires (1) a decision to change, (2) the courage to face the new feelings and take new actions, (3) a true desire to do whatever it takes without looking back, and (4) a professional coach or evaluator to keep you on track and give you viewpoints different from your own.

What I am saying here is that success, happiness and achievement are skills, and as such can be identified, taught and learned by anyone willing to pay the price of learning those skills.

Read the last paragraph again – it is accurate and true. We have clearly identified what it takes to grow the business or practice of your dreams and to live the lifestyle you want. The only roadblock is you, and how serious you are about changing and acquiring the personal ingredients that will propel you to your goals.

Success is not a strategy, it is an identity!

OUR MENTAL BLUEPRINT

Whether or not we realize it, we have within ourselves a mental blueprint of "who we are." It may appear to be vague or very general when we try to examine it. However, know that it is complete and exact down to the last detail.

This picture is a total summary of all that we believe. It is called our "self-concept" or "self-image." It pertains to every aspect of our being – our physical and mental characteristics, our abilities and talents, our hopes and dreams, virtually everything in our lives including the circumstances that surround us.

We have different concepts or pictures regarding ourselves in different situations. We may see ourselves as a superior athlete but a poor student, or a good parent but just an adequate son or daughter. There are thousands and thousands of different pictures stored in our brains.

These pictures are what we believe to be true about ourselves. They were formed unconsciously by our past experiences, our successes and failures, our triumphs and humiliations, what we read or observed, and to a great extent from what other people told us and how they reacted to us, especially in early childhood. This is environment conditioning and it did, like it or not, affect the way we think.

From all of this pre-programming, we formed a picture of the kind of person we are – and once that picture is formed, it becomes *true* as far as we are concerned. The situation may have been unavoidable, the data or input may have been totally in error, the incident may have been a freak occurrence – it does not matter.

Once we record the information, we do not question its validity. Many times we do not remember when or how we obtained the information. We act upon it as if it were, in fact, true.

The picture we have of ourselves becomes the key to our life.

All of our actions, feelings, behavior, even our abilities are always consistent with this picture. In short, we act like the kind of person we think we are. We cannot act in any other way. All of our will power, determination, and conscious effort will be to no avail. The success-striving mechanism within you will not have it any other way.

This is not a new idea. It has been discussed for thousands of years. King Solomon, whose name is synonymous with wisdom stated, *"What a man (or woman) thinks about, so is he (or she)."* Buddha said, *"All we are is a result of what we have thought."* The carpenter from Galilee simply stated, *"As ye believe, so shall it be done unto you."*

If you believe you are a failure, the built in GPS system within you will bring about the circumstances to prove it. If you believe yourself to be fat and see yourself that way, your internal navigation system will make sure you stay that way. You may be able to fight it consciously for a short time, but once you relax, the automatic guidance system will take over and put you right back where you believe you should be.

It is like a boat with an automatic pilot. If the autopilot is set to go north, you can take manual control of the steering wheel and turn west. But, as soon as you let go, the automatic guidance system will regain control and the boat will go north again.

All cases are not as clear-cut as the boat example. We are not always "going" or "not going" as the case may be. Sometimes we just speed up or slow down according to our present position and where our picture determines we should be. Our subconscious mind does not change the reality of the world around us; it just filters the information being presented in a way to support the present position of truth we hold in our minds.

For example, have you ever noticed that the mother of a new child can sleep through all kinds of disturbances such as the television, radio, cars and trucks going by, children playing in the neighborhood or myriad other noises? But, let her new baby utter a peep and she becomes aware and instantly awake. This is your filtering system at work. The subconscious mind filtered the information as unimportant to her until the baby cried. Then the recognition took place and the action followed.

Have you ever noticed that when you buy a new car, it seems that everywhere you look on the way home from the purchase there is a car just like the one you bought?

Everything within your line of vision is at all times being scanned by your subconscious mind for any item that is of interest to you. When you make an important decision like buying a car, the computer within you points out all the other cars similar to yours. It does this to support the decision you made by inferring, "You were right, they bought the same kind."

Not only will it point out things that support your decisions, but also it will avoid pointing out things that do not support your position of the truth. If you believe there is no opportunity for increasing your business, the success navigator within you will not point out new opportunities for increase.

Do not think that the success mechanism is designed to limit you. It is there to neither limit nor build you up. It just does whatever needs to be done to get you to the exact place you believe you should be. The super-conscious mind is neither good or bad, positive or negative! It is simply a computer that has been programmed and works to obtain the exact results of that program. It is results-oriented and goal-directed.

The super-conscious is a willing servant, never asking why, never questioning your choice, but carrying out orders you give it with unerring precision.

For example, if your self-talk is continually saying, "I catch one cold after another," your success mechanism will take these statements as truth and will conclude that is what you wish to experience. It will then set to work to produce that effect on the body.

If you think and believe that you are confident when meeting new people and that you always remember their names, your built-in computer goes to work again and takes your beliefs as truth. Then, when you meet new people you are poised, relaxed, self-assured and you will be able to remember their names.

The examples are endless. Your mental blueprint is complete down to the last detail and your internal software package is at all times bringing into your reality *the exact duplicate of the pictures you hold.*

Changing the Picture

The most exciting thing about your personal navigation system is that you can reprogram it. You can change the mental picture you have about yourself and actually change the results you are experiencing. No one is ever too young or too old to change the beliefs, concepts, or pictures they have.

One of the reasons that it has been so difficult for you to change your life significantly is that you have been trying to change the outer circumstances that surround you without changing the beliefs you have about those circumstances, your abilities and what you expect to happen. This is not merely positive thinking; positive thinking will not change the results we obtain with a poor self-concept.

The tools and techniques used to change one's self-concept are real and they work, *if* you trust them and believe they will work. What is important for you to understand now is that the results you obtain are in direct correlation to the thoughts, attitudes, and beliefs you developed throughout your life.

RETRAINING YOUR SUBCONSCIOUS MIND

W hen you learn how to retrain your subconscious mind, you will have the key to making your life whatever you want it to be, a key that nothing or no one can ever take away from you.

The power generated by your mind might well be the most important component in creating in your life all that you desire because everything begins in your mind. Remember the old saying, "That which you can conceive and believe you can achieve." This is not trite – it is the Law! There is no goal too big to be realized and no dream too big to be had – business or practice success, financial freedom, loving relationships, and even physical well-being. All things are possible IF you believe they are.

I am saying to you that the DOING and HAVING part of life doesn't get us to BEING anything. You cannot become happy, satisfied, loved, or successful simply by doing certain things. You can only BE when you come from BEING – being happy, being successful, being generous, being forgiving, being a loving person. You have to start there!

Another old saying states, "When you are up to your neck in alligators, it's hard to remember that you were there to drain the swamp." That's the way it is with life. When you are surrounded with problems in your business or in your private family life, it's hard to BE happy. It's hard to experience BEING, when the DOING and HAVING portions of you life are not working.

You and I have been so conditioned by our MFTPs that DOING and HAVING create BEING, that it becomes very difficult, virtually impossible at times, to BE anything, unless the DOING and HAVING portions are satisfied. Nevertheless, your pursuit of happiness and success will be much more enjoyable and you will "get there" faster and easier when you start with BEING.

In southern California there is a coastal aquarium where marine biologists are concerned with the intelligence of animal life in the sea. During an experiment a savage barracuda and a Spanish mackerel were placed in the same container with a glass partition separating them. Unaware of the transparent barrier, the barracuda quickly attacked the mackerel, but was stopped by the partition. After repeatedly bumping its nose, the barracuda finally quit trying. It had become conditioned to believe the barrier existed, even though it could not see it. After the actual barrier had been removed, the barracuda still could not get to the mackerel because it *believed* it was still there. Those two fish swam in the same tank for two years with only an imaginary barrier between them.

This is the same conditioning that you and I have been exposed to throughout our lives.

The main difference is that the initial barrier we experienced was probably not a real barrier like a glass partition, or a lid on a jar, or a small stake that holds a huge elephant in place, but one we were programmed to believe existed.

Many of the thoughts we have about our ability to be happy and successful in life have never been tested in the real world, yet we have imaginary barriers that hold us back. Too many of us seem to function based on the premise that the barriers are in fact real.

Be cautioned here! Do not waste your time debating about whether or not you are capable of a better business, getting a better job or having a more satisfactory personal life. *The whole point is that most of your limitations are self-imposed!*

You must admit that you have beliefs that have been programmed into you by your MFTPs and the environment. Well, get over it! The good news is, and we promise this to be true, that you can make your self-imposed barriers disappear and you do that by reprogramming your own subconscious mind.

Why bother? Because if you don't your environment and other people will have dominion over you and you will become their slave. Ridiculous! It is far better, we suggest, to design your own life and end up having whatever it is you want. Sure you can do it.

All you have to do is BELIEVE!

Some Great Beliefs

It would be incredibly powerful if you decided to develop a BELIEF SYSTEM with thoughts and concepts like:

1. I have the innate power to attract to myself anything I desire and want in my life!

2. What anyone else can do, I can do!

3. Everything in the realm of imagination IS in the realm of reality!

4. What I believe has a bearing on my success!

5. To be a "physical" success, I must first be a "mental" success!

6. Great people are just ordinary people with extraordinary determination!

7. You must change a flat tire with the same enthusiasm that you unwrap a gift!

8. From now on, decide to magnetize good things to you!

9. Anticipate the good, even during the bad!

10. Don't dwell upon what you don't have; concentrate on what you want to have!

11. Act one step bigger than you feel!

12. Don't allow anyone or anything to determine how you feel!

13. I love you, not because you are good, but because I am!

14. Act the part of the person you want to become!

15. Always keep problems and adversities in perspective!

    a. Kites fly against the wind.

    b. The stars shine brightest when the night is blackest.

c. Within every failure resides the embryo of an equivalent success.

16. Belief is the master; we are the slaves!

17. What you see is what you get!

18. I choose Circle – Circle!

SELF-AFFIRMATIONS

Whether you are conscious of it or not, you Talk to yourself constantly, either out loud where you can hear yourself, or silently, by thought, in your own mind.

Without realizing it, you either build yourself up or put yourself down all the time and, inadvertently, you are actually part of the cause of your own success or pain and poor self-image. If you constantly talk to yourself (repeat and review with regularity) over a long period of time, then your mind gets an image of what you want to create, and it does it for you without caring if it is good for you or bad, right or wrong. It just carries out your command as if you were the captain of the ship and you were giving orders to the crew. They too just carry out orders from above, whether they like it or not.

Affirmations are an act of confirming a statement of conviction. They declare the truth of something; they are a declaration of your approval and your assertion that you want something.

Sadly though, while affirmations are one of the best ways to program your mind to success, health, and happiness, many of the "self-affirmations" people use are negative in nature.

You put yourself down by making statements such as, I have no self-confidence, I am a procrastinator, I am afraid of (whatever the fear is), I feel guilty, That's just the way I am and I can't change, I can't control my temper, I look fat, I'm so dumb, I need eight hours of sleep to function, I am overwhelmed, I can't handle any more, I'm afraid to take risks, etc.

Negative self-affirmations are the negative beliefs you have about yourself and of which you remind yourself every day. They are negative statements about yourself, which sprinkle your everyday conversation. They are self-deprecating remarks that influence your behavior or beliefs and the negative descriptions given to you by your MFTPs when you were younger onto which you hold, even to this day.

Negative self-scripts are the negative self-images you have of your body, looks, weight, coloring, hair, or other parts of your body, which influence your feeling, and presentation of yourself to others. They are negative stories of your past behavior, humiliations, failures or performances that you systematically run over and over again in your mind and which now influences your current conduct.

And, although I can go on for pages and pages, I know you are getting the picture. So the last one I offer is the dread or fear you have of facing the future, the belief that you do not have what it takes to survive or to be successful in whatever circumstances you face. Wow, I'm exhausted. What about you?

The outcome of believing in negative self-affirmations can include lack of self-esteem and low self-concept, over-dependence on the approval of others, negativity, pessimism, self-pity and feeling like a victim, and the granddaddy of all, depression.

Please, Let's Turn Positive!

Positive self-affirmations are healing, positive self-scripts you give yourself to counter your negative self-scripts. They are vehicles by which you can free yourself from the dominion others have over you, and from their opinions, attitudes or feelings about you, allowing you to feel better about yourself.

Affirmations help you create the visualizations or a new order and sense in your life. They help you take personal responsibility for your own health and emotional stability. Self-scripts assist you in letting go of negative emotional baggage you have been carrying. Only then will you be able to deal with your life in a realistic and positive manner.

Self-affirmations help the resolution of feelings from the past so that you can face the present with a less obstructed view. In them you give yourself permission to grow, to change, to take risks, to rise up, and to create a better life for yourself.

Positive self-affirmations are for the recognition of your rights and affirming your claim on them, giving you an equitable chance of achieving your fullest potential.

And lastly, they are success prophesies that, when visualized, imagined or believed in, do come true.

Three Refreshing Self-Affirmations

Since 1980, I have never started any of my own seminars without asking the audience to stand up (some even got up on their chairs) and do an affirmation with me aloud, with energy and enthusiasm.

Following are three different ones that I wrote myself. Thousands around the world are currently repeating them, every day. The best time to do an affirmation statement is in the morning when you are too groggy to fight back with thoughts of lack and limitation.

Please do not read an affirmation with the speed and fluidity in which you generally speak or read something, even this book. Speak an affirmation out loud, slowly, and in a staccato-like fashion. Remember to emphasize the pronouns. Do it slowly and distinctly!

Affirmation 1

I am a healthy, vital, happy, and successful human being! I affirm this day that all tissues and organs in my body are functioning perfectly and that is the way it is supposed to be.

I am more relaxed than ever before because I choose peaceful loving thoughts and release my fears, worries, and anxieties. Tension is gone because I am creating an atmosphere of ease and confidence. My mind is uncluttered because I have set specific goals and planned action steps for their accomplishment.

I feel better now! Nature uses the food that I eat, the air that I breathe, the water that I drink and the rest that I get to rebuild, repair and revitalize me for the future. Radiant energy flows through me.

I also affirm this day that money is plentiful, in abundance and in unlimited supply. This money flows freely and constantly into my life as I render loving service to humanity. I have the right to be successful!

I prepare myself mentally and physically to attract everything that is necessary for my success. I accept this wealth because in my heart I am helping others regain their health, the most precious commodity. I gratefully and graciously accept this wealth and generosity from the universe.

On this day I give of myself unselfishly, extending my hand to help others. Opportunities to SERVE come continually and unexpectedly. My investments are wise and safe. I use my money to benefit not only myself, but others as well.

I choose to see good, hear good and do good for myself and all humanity. Happiness is part of my personality. I feel confident and secure, appreciated and loved, and therefore I am totally healthy, happy, and full of abundant life.

Affirmation 2

- I can do anything I want to do!
- I am doing what I love to do.
- I know whatever I need to know for my well-being, success, joy, and fulfillment!
- I am approaching my ideal weight, easily, naturally and permanently!
- I feel strong, confident, and worthy of success!
- I am magnetized to abundant health!
- I am a happy person!
- I love to laugh and enjoy life!
- I see good in every situation!
- I see abundance and opportunity at every turn!
- I take full responsibility for me!
- I am a good saver of money!
- I love getting out of debt!

- I am financially prosperous!
- I am rich!
- I am successful in everything I do!
- I am generous, kind, supportive, and compassionate!
- I give more than I receive!
- I have value as a person!
- I am professionally very competent!
- I am a magnet for all good things!
- I am strong and getting stronger!
- I love to give!
- I am a minister of encouragement...
  - A master of comfort to people...
  - A communicator extraordinaire...
- My potential is unlimited!
- I am my dream come true!
- I am wonderful!
- I am confident!
- I am self-assured!
- I am unique!
- I am worthy!
- I am wisdom!
- I am truth!
- I am beauty!
- I am wealth!
- I am harmony!
- I am courage!
- I am excitement!

- I am health!
- I am abundance!
- I am destiny!
- I am peace!
- I am successful!
- I am success!
- I am love!

YES, I CAN! YES, I WILL! YES, I AM!

Affirmation 3 (My Favorite)

I am here now! It is my intent to use this day to rebuild, repair, revitalize and refresh me for a more fulfilling, nourishing and satisfying life. My future is filled with abundant health, wonderful relationships, a thriving business, and financial freedom.

Today, and every day from now on, I will steadily shed ALL negatives and hurts from my past. I will override guilt, turn fear to faith, eliminate worry, and transform anxiety to calmness.

My ultimate goal is Personal Freedom! I give myself permission to grow, to take risk, and to create a better life for myself and my loved ones.

Every day, my connection with a higher source gets deeper, my inner strength grows stronger and I become peaceful and more at ease.

I am a good person. I am loving and courageous. I am caring and generous. I am trusting and open-minded and I have willingly selected to put myself on this new heroic pathway.

I now call upon the Law of Attraction to reach out and bring toward me all the opportunities and people necessary for me to continue my successful journey.

With faith and belief in a splendid future, I now devote myself to the fulfillment of my highest purpose.

Concepts, Thoughts, and Ideas to Reflect Upon as You Retrain and Reprogram Your Mind for Health, Wealth, Happiness, and Success

BEFORE "THE SECRET"

Long before the new international and phenomenally successful self-help book and documentary DVD entitled, *The Secret*, many of us in the personal growth industry, including me, wrote and taught our audiences similar concepts.

In fact, I have before me the first text I ever wrote way back in 1981. It was entitled, *The Philosophy, Business Acumen, Strategies, and Tactics Needed for Superior Professional Performance.* You can see from that title that in those early days of my career I focused in on the "Thoughts Create Reality" philosophy and coupled it with hundreds of action steps, lest those who were members of Markson Management Services thought that all they had to do was sit on a tufted pillow and play the flute and only good things would happen to them.

In *Bootcamp for Your Mind*, author Amy Applebaum says, "You don't get what you want just by sitting in a room and thinking about what you want. The key to all of this is action and your actions must be in alignment with your thinking. Without it you are sitting on the couch, dreaming up your life, but nothing is being created." Wow, the same stuff, reshuffled years and years later, but just as valid today as it was then.

In my text I wrote, "Whatever thoughts you fill your mind with and allow it to dwell upon will become your reality". Your unlimited power lies in your ability to control your thoughts. Remember that your life and the circumstances or things going on around you are a mirror of the thoughts that you allow to dominate your mind.

Sadly, throughout your life, you have been taught to concentrate on what isn't, what should be, what you don't have. You are continually bombarded by problem after problem. The news that starts and ends your day, the daily newspaper, the television shows you choose to watch are all inundated with the problems of the world – crime, corruption, disaster and poverty, etc.

Is it any wonder then that the majority of your thoughts are focused on your problems and the things you don't have? Or on those things that are going on OUTSIDE you? You have been taught that you need to concentrate on "fixing" everything, on the obstacles you must overcome. And, those thoughts just go out into the universe and attract back to you everything you don't want. What has actually happened to you or will happen to you is caused by what you were thinking about and what you acted upon.

Allow me please to remind you that, "What the mind believes, it acts upon, whether valid or not, whether good for you or not, whether beneficial to your future or not."

And your subconscious mind, which was programmed by the things you now think of or have thought of repeatedly in the past, is a willing servant, never questioning your choice, but carrying out the orders you give it with unerring precision.

Everything I have ever written about or taught is based on a few laws of physics. First, the granddaddy of all universal law, The Law of Cause and Effect, which says that what you put out, you get back. You create it and you get it back in direct proportion to the intensity of your thoughts and the actions you took.

Then there is the most powerful law of energy, The Law of Attraction, which simply says that "Like Attracts Like." Whatever thoughts you allow to dominate your mind, create the very things and circumstances you are thinking about. It works exactly like a magnet.

And finally, if you begin now to change the seeds you plant in your subconscious mind, you can change your entire future. And, that is the only way to do it. WE ARE WHAT WE THINK ABOUT! Short, simple, sweet, and elegant!

THE POSITIVE WORLD
OF SUCCESS

I am happy, successful, and enthusiastic! I feel great! I've got my life in order; it is working for my benefit – and you know what? It's WONDERFUL.

I challenge each of you reading this book to join with me, to get your life in order, to start moving toward more success, more happiness and more inner satisfaction and peace.

In order to start, you must first understand that success (health, wealth and happiness) is not a destination. It is, in fact, a journey that takes time. There is no "express" elevator to the top. Success is accomplished one step at a time, sometimes two, depending upon experience and attitude.

When we do achieve a level of success, we must not stop to bask in the glory of that achievement. We must move on, step by step, and climb higher and higher up the stairway until we reach the upper landing – our ultimate goal.

It is said, and it is true, that the only thing that is constant in nature is change. We cannot stand still or we will end up going backward. Our climb to the top of the stairway is accomplished by refining, growing, adapting, changing, and acquiring newer and more usable attitudes. The journey once begun is an exciting and fulfilling one.

Before you can manifest any degree of self-satisfaction, confidence, or greatness in your life, before you can acquire the physical things you desire, before you can own inner peace, before you can fulfill your destiny, you MUST change your inner thoughts and concepts.

There are success-type personalities and failure-type personalities, happiness-prone personalities and unhappiness-prone personalities. These personalities, in large part, are determined by your attitude. What happens on the inside reflects on the outside. Your present attitude is a reflection of who you are and where you are – right now!

If your attitude is poor, it must be corrected. If your attitude is fair, it has got to be improved. And, if you are already in possession of a good attitude, you've simply got to become more joyfully enthused. You must become totally committed to improving your life, instead of just passively participating in it.

All of your life, from birth to the present time, whether you are 6 or 60 years young, you have been living a life within the carefully dictated boundaries of morality, ethics, rights, wrongs, truths, lies, likes and dislikes.

The actual truth is that you have been pre-programmed to think and act (or more correctly, to REACT) to situations and challenges in your life like a robot. You never use the "freedom of choice" you were born with; rather, you allow the "compulsions of conformity" to dictate your action. You don't use your own powers because the same people who programmed you also informed, reinforced and led you to believe that "you can't do anything right."

They trained you to feel that you are slightly inferior and not quite as good as they are. You were taught, and you accepted as fact, that you can be anything you desire to be, as long as it was mediocre and average. Blend in with the crowd, be leery of others and their motives, justify and defend your position, hold on and be protective of your ideas and property – and think "doomy-gloomy" thoughts.

In reality, you have been subliminally brainwashed by people who unintentionally trained you to mirror their own low self-esteem. These very same people were carefully trained before you, by others who have in turn lost their minds to low self-esteem teachers – and the failure habit pattern develops, evolves and envelopes you, and then your children.

There is a better way to live. It's called the Positive World of Success. It is called "being in charge of your own life!"

YOUR SELF-FULFILLING PROPHECY

O ver and over again, I keep reminding you that, "The race is not won during the race; the race is won in the preparation of one's mind, body, and soul before the race begins!"

A successful business is never built during a busy day when the sheer volume of people to care for, paperwork to move, and business-related matters to deal with has you bobbing and weaving defensively. Success in business is built long before the "boss" gets to the office. The business builds as you prepare your mind, body, belief system, and delivery method, long before you actually get to the office. In fact, if you plan to win, if you have an attitude filled with positive expectations, and if you diligently practice your personal and professional skills, you will notice your life and career all being guided by your own self-fulfilling prophecy.

You can make the future anything you want it to be and regardless of all cynics, detractors, or doubters, you will find this "power" of self-fulfilling prophecy to be exhilarating when understood and purposefully used for your own benefit.

Superior athletes in all areas of sport know that mental preparation is just as vital to winning as physical fitness. I'm saying that how you think and visualize over a long period of time (mental preparation) is just as important as the physical things you do in your business environment. A "winning frame of mind" always precedes success and is clearly the difference between a high achiever and those who struggle but never quite seem to get there.

Over the years I have had the privilege of coaching thousands of self-confident, self-reliant people who predict the outcome of their personal plans and business efforts. It's something they have discovered inside themselves, and IT'S VALID!

Reduced to easy-to-digest terms, this validity encompasses how we think, what actions we take, what attitudes direct our actions, what expectations we hold for ourselves, what dreams we dream, and what goals or plans we set. In his classic book, *The Power of Positive Thinking*, by Dr. Norman Vincent Peale, he writes "When the mental picture of attitude is strongly enough held, it actually seems to control conditions and circumstances."

Remember, the laws that govern the action of your subconscious mind do not make choices as to right or wrong, good or bad. They act to give you what you think about the most, and that becomes your self-fulfilling prophecy. It is reported that prior to his death, Elvis Presley was consumed by the death of his dear mother who died when she was only forty-two. So did Elvis.

Former President Lyndon Johnson was convinced that he would not live beyond the age of sixty-three, because no male family member had ever exceeded that limit. And true to his expectations, he too died at sixty-three.

The other side works much the same way. Positive expectations, when they're held, thought about, and visualized over a long period of time, either consciously or subconsciously, affect attitudes and ATTITUDES INFLUENCE ACTIONS!

Making a conscious effort to create a self-fulfilling prophecy isn't difficult. It just takes a firm decision to control your own life. Think about that!! Controlling your own life! Powerful, isn't it? Maybe a bit scary too, but nevertheless, something that can indeed be accomplished with some determination, audacity, and just plain guts.

The key is that you must visualize what you want clearly, exactly, and in great detail. No dreaming, hoping, wishing, or speculation will ever work. Crystal clear pictures with emotion added when visualized again and again become tangible! If you make your visualized image clear enough, picture it vividly enough and believe in it sincerely enough, the infinite power of your mind will transform that vision into reality.

The only step left is that of affirming your implicit belief. Regular affirmations set the goal you have imagined. Your belief, hope, and expectation bring it to life. Reject all negative thoughts and actions by doing a positive affirmation each morning and evening and you'll love what will happen to you.

In the entranceway to The Success Motivation Institute in Waco, Texas, is a quoted sentence, spelled out in raised silver letters on a mahogany wall. It says, "WHATEVER YOU VIVIDLY IMAGINE, ARDENTLY DESIRE, SINCERELY BELIEVE, AND ENTHUSIASTICALLY ACT UPON MUST EVENTUALLY COME TO PASS!"

Given that truth, "Success Can Be Your Self-Fulfilling Prophecy."

PURGE YOUR BRAIN

Have you ever heard yourself say, "I'm spilling," or "I'm up to here," or "I can't take anymore." Sure you have, and so has everyone else.

Have you ever overloaded to the point that you wore yourself down emotionally, felt you had no room to put anymore in, and wanted to select flight instead of fight? Of course you have!

Did you ever get headaches from the seemingly endless lists of things to remember in order to be successful? Haven't we all. But how can that be when scientific studies all say that we only use a fraction of our brain capacity? How then can we overload so easily?

It sometimes seems that all the procedures, action steps, protocols, techniques, ideas, rules, habits, strategies, success acronyms and buzzwords pile up and you become frazzled and even paralyzed, not knowing what to do. And, I promise that booze or drugs are not the answer.

People run out of mental storage room for one of a few reasons. First, it is the way in which YOU view your own capacity. Instead of "I can't take it anymore," try the attitude that I and so many of our successful members have adopted, "Lay it on me, I can handle it all."

Secondly, overload comes from the erroneous belief that more is better, that if you only added one more new idea or one more action step it would all come together and the stress would disappear, which of course is not a valid belief.

Instead, what about purging your brain from once-valid beliefs and practices that have outlived their usefulness and applicability? What about taking some time to examine some of the misinformation or misconceptions that you've accepted as valid or true, but are not, and then purging them to make room?

For instance, I know a doctor who believed that if he lowered his fees he would attract more new patients and they in turn would refer more, stay longer, comply with his instructions better, be timelier, and bring flowers to his staff. A belief system such as that takes up as much room as a belief that says that patients are willing to pay a fair fee for a first-class, outstanding service and that by changing your attitude you can attract patients that are willing to stay, pay and refer regularly.

Excess mental baggage wears you down and piles up, not only affecting you, but negatively impacting your family, the people you work with and most importantly, it negatively affects the results you get.

We act on what we believe is true, whether it is true or not. Whatever we accept and believe determines how well what we do works because what we believe determines how we behave. And how we behave determines what we achieve or don't achieve.

Regardless of all the affirmations, goal setting and visualizations you attempt to do so diligently and regardless of all your good intentions, we are all susceptible to the Mother, Father, Teacher, Preacher-flawed thinking that eventually accumulates and leads to overload.

Dump this data from your memory banks and purge your brain. Forgive any past mistakes; forgive any petty or hard-line grievances that have been festering against others. Clean up your outside physical environment and free up some space for better, more positive and more productive alternative behaviors and actions.

Decide, right now, to walk away from anything, and I mean anything, that does not serve you, nurture you, or make you happy. Deliberately act AS IF you are not filled up, accept that you are responsible for creating the burdens you now carry, put a smile on your face, and make a decision to be free. Be Abraham Lincoln and free the brain slaves that chain you to mediocrity or unhappiness.

Like you purge your computer now to get rid of the old and make room for the new, do the same for your own personal built-in computer. Purge your brain, focus on what you want and not what you don't want, work on changing any ideas, actions, thoughts or beliefs that have proven to be counter-productive to your goals for success and happiness.

In short, clean it up, free it up, and move up!

THE YO-YO SYNDROME

If you are alive, there is a good chance that you are suffering from an infectious disease that is so highly contagious that it infects over eighty percent of the population. And once infected, there are various ways in which you are affected, largely based on your natural resistance to what your Mother, Father, Teacher and Preacher (MFTP) told you (in other words, how you were trained to think when you were young).

Some people suffer from only periodic and acute exacerbations of this disease, while others must deal with the more severe, chronic "Yo-Yoitis." The official Markson dictionary defines "Yo-Yoitis" as "a condition in which people experience tremendous emotional 'ups and downs' based upon what is happening to them in their businesses and personal lives."

If business is booming, they are elated beyond belief. They are UP! If, on the other hand, there has been no new business for a day or two, or, heaven forbid, a week, they immediately go down the tubes emotionally and even get depressed. They are DOWN!

They are UP when their businesses' numbers meet their goals and expectations and DOWN when the numbers drop even a few percentage points from the day, week or month before.

They are UP when the day is sunny, the sky is blue, the family is well, business is great and there is money in the bank and DOWN when it rains, plans have to be changed, things don't go as they anticipated and something costs more than they are willing to pay.

They are UP when the mail carrier delivers a big check and DOWN when instead of a check he or she delivers a late payment notice. UP and DOWN, UP and DOWN, continually UP and DOWN, like a yo-yo.

The Yo-Yo Syndrome is easy to diagnose. Symptoms usually include intermittent periods of elation and depression, happiness and frustration and, when severe, can even range from mild burnout to "Cranial-Anal Inversion." Yo-Yoitis destroys a person's supply of energy and enthusiasm like a never-ending roller coaster ride.

The ease with which this terrible condition can be observed and diagnosed comes from the fact that only outer-directed people are susceptible to this insidious disease. Outer-directed people are those who receive messages from the outside world regarding who they are on the inside. They allow *other* people, places, things, circumstances, or events to determine their feelings, their emotions, their reactions. They have a tendency to believe that inner happiness or success comes from the accumulation of money, objects, and trophies or by visible achievement and what others are thinking or saying about them.

In all cases, outer-directed people will find that the "self-worth" part of their self-image has been impaired. There is no centering, no higher purpose, and survival or winning is the ultimate goal.

Yo-Yo people are caught in a continuous loop of HAVE and DO, with little of no regard for BEING. They think, "If I DO this action step, then I should HAVE what I want, or in order for me to HAVE what I want, I'd better DO this or that." And around it goes, like an old-fashioned cassette tape, another version of UP and DOWN, of Yo-Yoitis.

With the Yo-Yo Syndrome, as with any disease process, it is best to correct the cause, rather than just ameliorate the symptoms. Symptom patching occurs naturally as the body attempts to heal itself via the quick-hit emotional highs garnered from victorious "outside" wins (achievement or recognition). Soon, if not constantly fed, the emotional UP fades and once the DOWN cycle starts again, one starts looking around on the outside to fix what is *broken on the inside.*

The cause of Yo-Yo Syndrome is located above your eyes and between your ears in that amazing memory bank called your brain. The good news is that now that we have located where the problem is, with time and some effort on your part, it can be removed without drugs or surgery.

When you discover your essential nature and learn who you really are on the "inside," you will come to realize that Yo-Yos are always influenced by "outside" situations, circumstances, and things that just seem to *happen to you.*

Your behavior in those cases is generally fear-based. It comes from a need for external power, a need for personal approval and acceptance, a need to control your outcomes. That's why you are UP when things go your way and DOWN when you don't achieve the results you desire.

When you are UP you take the credit, but when you are DOWN you either rationalize why something didn't go right or you tend to blame and lay the cause of the failure on others.

So, how do you stop the Yo-Yo, the ups and downs based on the things that happen to you? The answer is really easy to describe, but more difficult to correct because of the habitual nature of the problem and the way we have been taught to think.

The cure for the Yo-Yo Syndrome lies in working on the personality traits within you. On the positive side are the inner characteristics of love, faith, belief, honesty, ethics, confidence, generosity, forgiveness, courage, determination, commitment, discipline, respect, kindness, truthfulness, and humor.

On the negative side of personality characteristics (those which cause the downs) are fear, criticism, envy, jealousy, blame, laziness and procrastination, hatefulness, being judgmental, sarcasm, cowardliness, clutter, frugality, doubt, compulsiveness and dishonesty.

When *you decide* to become loving, trusting, non-judgmental and of high purpose, you will immediately discover your innate creativity and incredible potential to manifest all you want – and get it with effortless ease. Then the Yo-Yo Syndrome will disappear forever!

WHY POSITIVE THINKING WORKS

Often I hear uninformed people say things like, "Positive thinking is fine, but it does not reflect reality. It's too Pollyanna." Ouch! Nothing could be further from the truth, but that's how some people really feel.

My thinking is that while this may be a common accusation, it is dangerously naïve and harmful. If ninety percent of what we worry about never happens, how is negativity more realistic than being in possession of a positive mental attitude? The fact is that what is indeed realistic is up to us, depending upon how we shape our own thoughts.

A positive mindset will not save you from bad news, but your reactions to bad news are under your control. Remember, it is not how you act that determines how successful you will be. It is how you *react*, especially to bad news, that determines who you are.

When someone says anything that jolts you or hurts your feelings in some way, you can either select to react and feel badly about yourself or you can say aloud or to yourself, "That is simply your opinion." A self-explanatory example could be when someone says something unkind or cruel to you like, "I don't like that shirt you are wearing." You can feel bad and go and change your shirt, allowing someone on the outside determine how you feel on the inside. Or you can smile with confidence and a positive attitude and say, "That is simply your opinion!"

Positive thinking works, but only when Repeated and Reviewed with Regularity (RRR), and it must be practiced all the time. Repeat, Repeat, and Repeat it again! This is not trite! It is, in fact, what makes the difference between people and the results they get in life.

I am not just speaking about simple and silly things like the shirt example we just reviewed. I am speaking about serious issues as well, like when someone gets cancer. I am thoroughly convinced that positive thinking makes all the difference in the world with regard to the recovery rate. At least, that was my own experience.

Every day needs to start off in a positive way or with a preplanned program of daily positive input. You can select a simple positive statement or a one-line affirmation, but it you must do it every day, immediately after you open your eyes, before you are too groggy to fight back with thoughts of lack and limitation.

It amazes me that most of the people who are stuck-in-their-stuff seem to feel that a program of daily positive energizing is optional. They are wrong. Success is NOT optional. It should be a mandatory study undertaken by all human beings who are serious about making their lives better.

Your brain REQUIRES constant positive input, just like a plant requires constant water and nourishment. You need to build a collection of inspirational books and CD albums and read or listen to them daily. The effect will probably be greater than you think possible, both on yourself and on the world you inhabit.

Positive thinking is the catalyst that causes you to shift and to replace some of the "stinkin' thinkin'" that has been embedded in your subconscious mind over the years.

Simply put, I want you to stop thinking and talking negatively; it cannot help you in any way. And while you are at it, stop putting yourself down, stop complaining at any cost, stop associating with anyone who does not make you feel better about yourself, stop giving others permission to keep you from being great, stop being timid, stop whining and instead go the opposite way.

Remember – your mind reacts to what it is fed, whether it is true or false. Make it true, make it positive, make it magnetic and energetic, and allow your positive thinking to create your new reality.

I GUESS I AM TOO COMFORTABLE

Often when I ask why someone thinks they are stuck in one place, or on a plateau of one kind or another, or not growing in any aspect of their lives or practice, they are silent for a moment and then in a low tone they end up saying something like, "I guess I am too comfortable."

Ugh! My usual reaction is generally to close my eyes, look down to the ground, take a deep breath and let out an audible sigh, before I lift my eyes to be sure I have solid contact with theirs and ask (sometimes with a bit of a tone, I must admit), "And just what does being comfortable have to do with success?"

Figuratively speaking, how does sitting under a blanket, on a tufted couch, in front of a fireplace contemplating what you are not doing well comfort you? And what does that have to do with correcting the issues (that way down deep you know are there) that are holding you back from becoming all that you want to be?

Comfort is indeed a warm and fuzzy feeling and while there are indeed times to just kick back, hang out, laze around and get comfortable, that is not what we are talking about here, and you know it.

This is not just about being uncomfortable. We are talking about your desire to avoid attempting something because you do not want to fail or because you are afraid of criticism or rejection. Take a risk, confront, and get into the action.

Whew! That is a mouthful and a lot to digest. I know from my experience as a coach that if I do not put you in a place you find uncomfortable or encourage you into an uncomfortable place, *you will not grow!* Ultimately, you must resolve the reasons, alibis, excuses, rationalizations, and defense mechanisms that you have habitually used to feel safe and comfortable so you can grow.

Wanting to be comfortable at any cost, costs confidence, success, prosperity, happiness and fulfillment. How does that feel? Is it too high a price? I think so, and I am sure you do too.

So, what to do? In fact, the second most common question I get all the time (the first is, "How do I get more new business?") is, "Larry, what do you think I should do?" I'd rather you ask who should I be or become, but I will attempt to give a good answer to a poor question. And the answer is: learn to deal with and overcome your fears. That is what you are hiding from when you want to be comfortable. The six basic fears are fear of the unknown, abandonment, loss, rejection, failure, and success. Of course, each of these has many subheadings, such as fear of criticism, risk, embarrassment, death, ill health, and poverty.

Remember, too, that most of the fears you face do not belong to you in the first place. They are passed on to you from your Mothers, Fathers, Teachers, or Preachers and although grown now, you chose to keep them. Basically, you are either aligning yourself with a parent's (good or bad) characteristics or running from them and going the opposite way.

For example, imagine that your father was a controlling person who consumed all the space and made all the decisions for people, whether they liked it or not. You either emulated and modeled him (to get his love and attention), becoming like him, or you ran from him because you hated the feeling he gave you and became a non-confrontational peacemaker afraid of taking a leadership role.

The cure is to embark upon a serious program to deal with the fears, neutralizing them and turning them into great assets for your growing confidence and success.

WOODROW WILSON UNDERSTOOD!

Woodrow Wilson, the twenty-eighth president of the United States (1913 – 1921), once said, "You are not here merely to make a living. You are here in order to enable the world to live more amply, with greater vision, with a finer spirit of hope and achievement. You are here to enrich the world, and you impoverish yourself if you forget the errand."

Hmmm – while that was written about eighty-eight years ago, no doubt it could be included into any speaker's platform as they ramble on about high performance and human potential. This statement is so powerful that I don't want it to get lost here, relegated to being another seemingly insignificant, positive-thinking, fill-the-space blurb we all use in our writings and presentations.

Instead, let's examine what it says. First, "You are not here merely to make a living," and while the vast majority of uninformed people *do not know that*, it is the bitter truth. They believe that making a living is what it is all about and nothing could be farther from the truth. Just making a living is survival thinking at best and indicates relegation to a lifetime struggle just to keep up.

Merely making a living generally indicates a mediocre existence, a "sameness," a safe routine with nothing changing over time, a stuck-in-your stuff attitude. Surely, just getting by does not scream the excitement, happiness, fulfillment or energy that comes by setting high standards, lofty goals and taking massive action steps. Remember, we were born to look up, look ahead, and move forward.

The next sentence of Woodrow Wilson's quote, "You are here in order to enable the world to live more amply, with greater vision, with a finer spirit of hope and achievement" seems to me to be self-explanatory, except for the fact that it is sneakily powerful. When we break it apart a bit we find, "To enable the world to live more amply," which is a phrase that speaks of universal potential, of abundance and of generosity.

And how about, "with a greater vision?" This has always been and always will be the key to success, positive change, and growth. A vision, a concept, an idea, or future thought that when put into action creates targets that result in expansion and new applications.

That sentence ends with Wilson saying, "with a finer spirit of hope and achievement." This is truly the magic of the sentence – without hope all is lost.

Hope stirs the pot of human potential by saying that there is a dream of more, of bigger, of better. There is a chance to grow, for things to get better and for achievements that, though maybe not possible at the moment, are inevitable in the future.

And finally, Wilson ends with, "You are here to enrich the world, and you impoverish yourself if you forget the errand." Yes, you are here to do your part, to contribute and to enrich, not only yourself and others, but to make larger, more altruistic contributions to humanity at large – to share, to give back to the source and to something greater than yourself, to help, to venture forth, to love!

"And you impoverish yourself if you forget the errand" is the lesson of the universe. It says that you are expanding or shrinking, moving forward or backward, giving or taking. Forget that mission in life and you will end up poor of spirit, of mind, of body and of purse.

Yes, yes, yes: "You are not here merely to make a living. You are here in order to enable the world to live more amply, with greater vision, with a finer spirit of hope and achievement. You are here to enrich the world, and you impoverish yourself if you forget the errand."

BEHAVIOR NEVER LIES

A while back, I had the pleasure to play a round of golf with a good friend and one of my personal mentors, the one and only Richard Flint. During the wonderful day we spent together, Richard told me that he had written a new book entitled, *Behavior Never Lies*.

Shortly thereafter, Richard was a Celebrity Guest Speaker at one of my seminars. In his presentation he elaborated on his Behavior Never Lies theme. Personally, I was totally engaged and found myself magnetically drawn to what he was saying. Perhaps that was because it paralleled so many of my beliefs and teachings over the years.

Yes, your behavior outwardly vividly displays WHO YOU ARE inside your skin. Your behavior shows others, and, if you are observant enough, gives you great feedback as to your own concepts, thoughts, and feelings. Additionally, your behavior brings to life your character traits, your strengths, weaknesses, securities, insecurities, likes, dislikes, especially when you are not on guard. It even openly shows others the mood you are in.

That's what he means by your behavior never lies. Actually, it reveals who you are, good or bad, and is a great mechanism that you can use to become aware of some of the weaknesses you have and the areas of personal growth that require some attention.

For example, if you are a person who fears rejection, then your emotional withdrawal or negative feelings when someone ends a relationship with you will be displayed by your behavior. That feeling just points out your weak area, the one that needs work. And, by the way, ignoring the issue doesn't make it go away. Sooner or later, you will come to understand that once you identify a weakness, it is incumbent upon you to do whatever it takes to turn that weakness into strength. The end result is, of course, a growing confidence and an improved self-image that dramatically changes your focus, power of attraction and ability to move forward.

Is it the automobile that inadvertently cuts you off while driving that gets you angry and all bent out of shape, or is it the anger that was residing within you that was brought to the surface by the traffic incident? Your behavior proved it. The reason for your anger was not caused by the other guy; it was caused by harboring an anger characteristic that needed attention. What you impress on the inside, you express on the outside.

The more work you need to do in a particular area of your personality, the more your behavior will prove to you that you need to change.

Remember, this works both ways. Your behavior will also show you and others the good characteristics that you possess. For instance, it is easy to see someone who loves animals – just watch their face when they see a puppy. People who love children squeal with delight when they see a newborn and every one of your family, friends and employees know from your behavior if you are generous or cheap, warm and kind, or hard and bully-like. I am asking you to use your behavior as a barometer of who you are.

Use the Behavior Never Lies mechanism to help you make serious and important decisions about the areas that needed attention, and then decide to change, set some goals, take some action and enjoy a newer and better you.

HOW TO ATTRACT SUCCESS

The title says, "How to Attract Success." This is a subject that I will be happy to discuss with you, but first, why don't I give you what I perceive to be a pretty good definition of someone who is a success.

A success is anyone who is deliberately doing a predetermined job because that's what he or she decided to do. And by the way, that is only a small fraction of the population. Meaning, if I *decided* to do something, if I gave my word, if I told myself that this is what I wanted to accomplish, that is what I will do, no choice, no doubt about it.

Also, I believe that success is predetermined by your faith, confidence and belief in your product, services, and ideas, or as Dr. Jim Parker used to say, "Your FCB in your PSI."

Success does not come to you from the outside. It comes to you from the inside and since who you are (your thoughts, your feelings, your attitudes, your skills, your character, your energy field, your desire, your focus, your purpose and all your actions) attracts to you every single ingredient you require for success, you could say that success is indeed attracted to you.

The *how to attract success* secret is to learn that it is you that attracts or repels the people, the situations, the opportunities, the circumstances and the events that provide the team who makes the plan and puts it into effect.

And if your thoughts create your reality, which they do, then it can be said that your thoughts become things. And if that is true, which I promise you it is, then your thoughts (conscious and unconscious) provide the catalysts for your success – or your failure.

The most important factor in attracting success is to develop a belief system that is indelibly inscribed in your soul, one that does not move with the wind, bend with the circumstances or get changed by others' influence.

Here are some belief systems that I have learned over the years. First, what someone else has done, others can do. Meaning, if others have become successful, then it is possible for you to become successful, too. You see, what you believe has a bearing on your success and everything in your imagination is in the realm of possibility.

I have also come to know that to be a physical success, you must first be a mental success and that great people are just ordinary people with extraordinary (even better, extra-ordinary) determination.

How about expecting a miracle every day, acting one step bigger than you feel, and anticipating the good even through the bad?

What about changing a flat tire with the same enthusiasm as you would unwrap a gift, and decide not to dwell on what you don't have and concentrate hard on what you want?

Here's one that I have, over the years, made part of my own mantra collection. It says, "From now on I am going to magnetize good things to me." I say it over and over to myself every day. "Today I am going to magnetize good things that will flow into my life."

The bottom line is that you must have the audacity to seek success and that you attract success into your life by being the best you that you can possibly be. Remember, you attract into your life your feelings, so what I did, and what I am asking you to do is to deliberately develop a belief system that emanates out from you into the universe, and allow that belief system the time to bring back the keys that unlock the vault to greatness and success.

TURNING IT ALL AROUND

Recently I received an email from a member of Markson Management Services of more than ten years ago. In that communication he said that he was always interested in my stories of the days where I experienced lesser success, which I guess was a kind way of saying my failure days. He asked how I turned it all around, what triggered my new mindset that resulted in greater success later on. And, lastly, he said he remembered me saying that pure positive thinking, by itself, never works.

Even after all these years, it's easy for me to remember what triggered the mindset for my turnaround – and as much as I would like to tell you that my motivation was pure and well intentioned, that would be a lie.

My original motivation, sad to say, came from the jealousy I had seeing others experience more success and happiness than I was experiencing. It came from fear that people would see me as the loser I was. And it came from internal pain and from a self-image that told me I was simply not good enough.

What event prompted my turnaround? Remember the seminar I described at earlier in the book? If a great friend hadn't paid my way, the single most important event in my life never would have happened.

To make a long story short, based upon what I learned at that seminar, I made a decision to change my life. I started doing an affirmation each and every morning; I wrote goals for the first time in my life; I started to copy, mimic, plagiarize and steal the attitudes, actions and procedures of anyone who was more successful than I was, which was everyone, and that kept me quite busy for a long, long time.

I put a smile on my face every day, changed how I greeted people, shook everyone's hands, and gave them a compliment. I looked them in the eyes for the first time in my life and acted as if I were already successful.

I became positive, focused, energetic, and action-oriented. I changed my office hours, my fees, the speed with which I worked. I even spoke a little louder and a little more enthusiastically to everyone I communicated with.

I gave real recommendations to patients, no longer letting them get away with what they wanted – inferior, but quicker and cheaper health care. I began to police their visitation schedules and no longer allowed them to come or go when their pain went away or when their insurance went away.

You might say I found the guts and audacity to tell them the truth and not buckle to what they wanted – one magic treatment, instant cure, with no charge and put it in the mail so they were not inconvenienced by coming to the office.

I began to be more thankful and gracious and generous. I was actually feeling more confident and the results were truly amazing. It was like turning on a faucet of new patients, better friends, and more opportunity. The more I changed, the better things became, and I finally learned to stop complaining and blaming others for the cause of my own misery.

Then I modernized my office, updated my equipment, and started to pay attention to details, including sending out a minimum of three thank you notes each and every day to anyone who gave me great service. I even sent notes to my patients telling them that I appreciated them and wished all my patients were as nice and cooperative.

Instead of my heretofore normal *poor little unfortunate me mantra* I had used to help myself fail, I chose to develop and use only two things – optimism and action!

Hopefully, those who are struggling a little will get this message. It is NEVER too late to become more successful and if I can do it, YOU can do it too!

EMOTIONS OVERCOME LOGIC

A while back I spent a wonderful hour on the telephone, speaking with a very smart professional woman who is a successful attorney. She was, at the time, also registered for one of my upcoming Cabin Experiences.

She and I had never met and my only live contact with her before was when she first registered for The Cabin Experience. She was upbeat, inquisitive and had high expectations of the benefits of participating in a Breaking Free – Personal Freedom Retreat of this kind.

This time though her attitude was different. It was prompted by a recent turn of events that was putting so much financial pressure on her that she was considering dropping out of The Cabin Experience so she could save the money. I could hear the angst, the pain, and uncertainty on the phone and, just like a common pattern I often witness, this normally positive woman sounded scared and afraid.

So, we scheduled the one-hour consultation. It's purpose was not to talk her into changing her mind and coming to The Cabin Experience, but rather to hear her "story" (yes, everyone of us has a "story" to tell, especially when things go wrong), and see if I could be of assistance in changing her perception and the choices she was making.

When a person goes into fear (which is an emotion, of course), all logic flies out the window and the victim either looks for something or someone to blame or, worse yet, they blame themselves.

During her story she revealed that she had exhausted her savings to buy the home of her choice and relocate her professional office out of a building she owned, leaving the existing tenants to pay the mortgage. As it turned out, a few of them didn't renew their leases and one major tenant who rented a large space moved out.

I am sure that none of us would be happy if that happened to us and probably all of us would have some concern if we were in the same position. But, I am also sure that each of us would REACT differently to the same circumstances. Some would panic, flame the fires of the poverty and self-worth issues yet unresolved within, while others would select different thought processes and actions – and life would go on.

Interestingly enough, as this very bright and intelligent woman told her story, I observed the tone of her voice, the emotion, the fear, and the fact that she was constantly putting herself down and that she dreaded the future.

She kept saying things like, "I made stupid decisions; I am very worried and money is so tight; I just don't know what I will do. I have no money saved; I need to get more tenants immediately. I need to get more clients." And around it went like a hamster on a wheel. Then the final touch, "I can't even sleep because my mind keeps going over this stuff again and again."

Pray tell, how exactly does this kind of thinking, emotion and negative self-talk help solve the problem? Or is it this kind of thinking (even if it was hidden in the subconscious mind) responsible for attracting all the problems in the first place? Something to ponder, I think you would agree.

Remember, *you attract into your life your feelings* and, therefore, you must, by choice, regardless of circumstances, purposely select thoughts and feelings that move you away from your pain and paint the picture of the solution you want to experience. Would she starve to death if no one rented the space or was she just planting those seeds in her mind?

Well, after I listened carefully and paid close attention to the details of her story, I started to give her a list of better choices she could make and the self-talk she could inculcate into her daily routine.

We talked about what she would feel like if all her problems were solved, as if by magic. We talked about positive outcomes and lofty dreams. We spoke about wonderful relationships, a thriving practice, an abundance of money. We created scenarios of happiness and fulfillment, and what do you think happened?

Yes, one hour later I was speaking to an entirely different person. This "new" woman seemed to be gathering courage, appeared to be unafraid and ready to face up to the past and create the actions that would build a better future. She was turned around – and we were both thrilled.

And, by the way, she did not withdraw her registration for The Cabin Experience.

THE MASTERMIND PRINCIPLE

When I began exploring success, way back when, one of the first books I read was Napoleon Hill's all-time classic, *Think and Grow Rich.* It was a book that literally changed my life (still available on Amazon.com), for in it Napoleon Hill elaborated on "The Mastermind Principle," The premise is that a group of positive, like-minded individuals can help each other reach goals they could never achieve by themselves.

The Mastermind Alliance is a subject that I worked on understanding for many, many years. In fact, in answer to the age-old question, "What did you do to become so successful?" I promptly answer that I became expert in "The Mastermind Principle of Success," and that over the years I made a concerted effort to surround myself with a small synergistic group of the most positive, most focused, most energetic, best thinkers I could find.

For years, I participated in a Mastermind Alliance with seven other men and women. We met, no matter what, every other Monday evening for three or four hours.

Later, in the Markson Management Services and Masters Circle days, I brainstormed with the officers or partners every single week. We set goals, held ourselves accountable, reviewed what had happened, what was currently going on, and talked about the future. We added, subtracted, deleted. We laughed, we cried, we agreed, and we disagreed -- but collectively we dreamed and planned, and we moved forward!

Being aligned with a Mastermind Group, Club, or Alliance is, in my opinion, an essential tool of success. A Mastermind with the right kind of like-minded people can be priceless, and it can open doors far beyond anything you can even imagine.

The Mastermind experience itself is an exhilarating, stimulating, provocative, and continuous collaboration that allows you to forge new strategies, uncover shortcuts, make seemingly insurmountable problems disappear and help you create new opportunities to enlarge your concepts and visions.

Mastermind Alliances rekindle passion and purpose, reignite internal fires, and reanimate the spirit - and if all of the above isn't enough, it gives you an opportunity to break bread with and get to know others up close and personal.

A while back, I received an email from Jay Abraham, nationwide marketing and success guru. In it Jay, without knowing it, sums up my thinking perfectly. He says, "Unless and until you surround yourself with like-minded people who will generously and collaboratively hold each other to a higher standard...with a seasoned coach/leader to nurture and support you and hold you accountable, as well as, to provide direction - you will never be working at the highest levels of your performance capability. You will plateau, atrophy, regress and worse...you will be settling for far less than you can have, be or do in life and in practice." Wow, how can I say that better?

Work on joining or creating a Mastermind Alliance of your own. All you need is a burning desire to grow yourself and your practice/business/personal life and to hang out with the best of the best. The effort will be worth it, I promise.

SELF-CONFIDENCE

Yes, self-confidence – a word that we hear every day and even acknowledge as being a terrific characteristic of a personality. Yet it is a word that is often misunderstood. Self-confidence is definitely one of the major catalysts for success and the antithesis of the demon called fear.

Self-confidence is an internal mindset that grows by having the right attitude to begin with and then it is fostered by all the achievements that come as a result. Self-confidence on the inside is displayed and visible on the outside by courage, guts, audacity, determination, and action.

Self-confident people have the feeling that they are indeed worthy of success and not the feeling that always questions whether they are worthy enough to achieve anything.

In my experience with thousands of clients who are in the process of growing their confidence, which is a good thing, I have noticed that all of them have come to know that if something they do is ill-conceived or they actually fail at a task – they NEVER view themselves as a failure.

It becomes okay for them to say, "Wow, I certainly screwed that up," or "I got that wrong," or "It failed because I either didn't know enough, or spend enough time with it, or wasn't diligent enough," – whatever – BUT, they also feel or say, "I am not a failure because what I attempted to do failed."

That is huge and applies to all the failures in your life – from failing a test to failing at a business venture or a marriage or at a sporting event, everything you have failed at.

Self-confident people have a righting mechanism, much like a cat that always lands on his feet. Only in their case, the righting mechanism causes them to take an optimistic approach – one that says, "Yes, that took some time or cost me some money and I got it all wrong, but if I blame myself, put myself down and fret over the results, it will, if repeated enough, cause me to create a fear that could stop me in the future. Instead, I fully acknowledge the failure and the fact that I was responsible, but I intend to stand up every time I am knocked down, and I will start over again – on this or any other project that I deem important."

Some lessons that I have learned:

1. If you think you can't win, you won't

2. If you think you will lose, you've already lost

3. If you believe that you are not worthy, the things that will happen to you will prove that you were right

4. If you think all rich people are thieves, you will never achieve financial prosperity

5. If you look in the mirror and find yourself unattractive, that is how others will view you too

6. If you are afraid and procrastinate, opportunities will pass you right by, but you won't even know it.

7. If your self-talk is negative, you are sure to attract negative circumstances into your life.

On the other hand, if you grow your self-confidence and come to think or better yet believe:

1. That if he or she can do it, so can I

2. That my confidence will cause something great to happen to me today

3. That I believe it is possible to create my life's dreams

$. That I am worthy of success

5. That I can handle all challenges that come my way

6. That I will stand up one more time than I am knocked down

7. That Success comes To you, not From you.

Finally, remember that others will believe in you when you believe in yourself. They will "tune in" on your thoughts and feel toward you just as you feel toward yourself. That is because your behavior literally broadcasts your self-confidence.

Act like you are self-confident until it becomes a habit. You will love the results.

PROCRASTINATION

I will bet you it is one of those things that grab you on a consistent basis. It is an everyday part of life. You know it is a challenge; you talk about needing to stop doing it, but it is still there staring you in the face and causing turmoil in your life. What am I talking about? That thing called Procrastination!

Do you ever find yourself challenged by it? How many stacks do you look at before you give yourself permission to just leave them there? How many conversations have you had with yourself and with others about the fact that you need to stop your procrastinating? Some of you have even made your need to stop procrastinating one of your New Year's Resolutions.

Do you realize what Procrastinating does to you? As long as you procrastinate, you must repeat yesterday.

Procrastination will:

- Provide you with emotional challenges,
- Open you to unnecessary conflict,
- Compound confusion,
- Refuse to allow you to grow,

- Allow negative space,

- Steal from others,

- Take respect away from you,

- Increase your personal stress,

- Negate the good that might be happening,

- Alter the journey,

- Test your level of commitment, and

- In the long run, exhaust you.

Can you see that procrastination will keep you from moving forward? It is important that you understand that procrastination is a by-product. It is not a stand-alone behavior. It is the result of your top enemies coming together – confusion creates fear, which results in doubt, that creates disorganization, that steals your desire, which drains your spirit. When this happens, you will find yourself staring off into space, lacking energy, and you will most certainly begin to procrastinate.

Have you ever lived this way? How many times has your procrastination just added to your stress?

The question is, *How do you control the behavior of Procrastination?* Understand, you will never completely eliminate procrastination, but you can control your tendency to procrastinate.

To control procrastination:

- Completion must be the crusade.

  - *What you don't complete has continuation.*

- Organization must be in place.

  - *Without organization, you will be scattered.*

- Never create stacks.
  - *Stacks steal energy and leave you empty.*

- Time must be respected.
  - *Time is consistent, you are not.*

- Refuse to live in tomorrow.
  - *Tomorrow is an illusion you don't have.*

- Open yourself to help.
  - *Without help, you will lack clarity.*

- Look at the depth of your commitment.
  - *Your commitment defines your desire.*

Procrastination is a choice. Simply stated, procrastination is the behavior of avoidance. Anything you avoid doesn't go away; it just creates another emotional stack that keeps stealing energy. It creates that mental question, "When are you going to go back and complete what you started?" Anything that is not completed has continuation. It is the continuation that steals your focus, steals your energy and makes it okay to wait!

If you really are serious about improving your life, make waiting an *unacceptable behavior*.

*****

Note: Procrastination was written by my great friend and international personal development guru, Richard Flint. It recently appeared in his wonderful monthly Mindjogger Newsletter, and I thought it was so important that I wanted share it with you. It is reprinted here with his permission.

PLAY TO WIN FROM WITHIN

When I founded Markson Management Services, it was a Strategy-Based company; it was all about what members should DO. Years later, when I realized that I could teach all the right strategies for success, but that some were still unable to reach their goals, I shifted the paradigm and began to use an Identity-Based approach. That meant that who a person was inside their skin (their thoughts, actions and feelings) dictated what they would or wouldn't do.

And even though our primary focus at the time was teaching the latest and best procedures, I discovered that success was "All In Your Head", meaning inside your brain and not necessarily coming from the action steps alone.

Success is an abstract thing – it is between your ears and it is not about action alone. A four-billion-dollar self-help industry provides proof that "you attract your feelings into your life," that "thoughts become things" and that "what goes around comes around."

In those early days, I hired some fabulous guest speakers to deliver that message, knowing that famous "experts" from out of town would grab clients' attention faster and better than I could. One of my all times favorites was Brian Tracy, one of the most prolific and successful high-achievement and human potential coaches in the world. In fact, I believe his all-time best selling album, *The Psychology of Achievement*, was and still is at the top of my all-time best list.

Not very long ago I had the pleasure of meeting Janet Attwood, the co-author, with her husband, Chris, of a great book entitled, *The Passion Test*. What caught my attention was an interview that Chris had conducted. Here are the key lessons from this interview about living your passion, just what I have been speaking about for years.

1. It is never too late to discover your passion. Most multimillionaires are made after the age of fifty.

2. Successful people achieve their greatness because they have something to express inside. They are motivated by the desire to produce the very best that is inside them.

3. Talent and passion are the twin towers of success.

4. It isn't always talent that creates passion. Sometimes passion uncovers talent.

5. Sometimes the passion to overcome something we're trying to make up for uncovers our talent.

6. The things you loved to do as a child provide clues to your natural talents.

7. Find ways to save people time and money and give it to them the way they want it – Michael Dell's secrets to success.

8. Time management: What routines am I going through that are a total waste of time and are not leading me toward the achievement of my goals?

9. We all live in our imaginations and are caught in the world between our ears. We create our world outside from what we are doing inside.

10. When things are not going well, you need to replay your success and then project in your imagination where you want to be. The mind can't distinguish between simulated activity and real activity.

11. Create the habit pattern and experience of a winner inside, so when you get there on the outside, it's like old home week. It feels so comfortable to succeed because you've been through so many dress rehearsals.

12. Believe you are as good as the best, but not better than the rest.

13. Failure is a detour, not a dead end. It is the fertilizer of future success.

14. Your self-worth will determine your eventual net worth. You will earn and accumulate what you believe you are worthy of having.

There you have it in a tidy little nutshell. Enjoy!

THE POWER OF OBSERVATION

One of the essential ingredients to success is one that is rarely spoken about at seminars and even in myriad self-help books that flood the market on a daily basis. The ingredient that I am speaking about was, while I was in practice, and still is today, one that I credit for allowing me to succeed in business and life, for all of these years – and it is NOT to be underestimated.

What is this characteristic? It is *observation*! Better said, it is "The Power of Observation." This is a skill that can be practiced, learned, and put to work on a regular basis.

You have probably noticed that some people are more observant than others – they just seem to have a keener eye and are more aware of what is going on around them. Some can walk into an overly-cluttered room and not seem to notice, while others see it immediately. Some are aware of the visual landscape, the sounds and aromas around them – others seem oblivious. Some notice clothing, body language and posture, facial expressions, tones of voice, the ambiance of the moment, and even, when expert, pick up how people form their sentences, their congruency and intent.

Wow! What a powerful tool. Can you imagine your increased power if you became a truly observant person and used that skill (natural or acquired) to help you make important distinctions?

The distinctions made from your observations can be used to help you mirror and model, or as I like to say, "mimic, copy, plagiarize and steal the attitudes, actions and procedures used by those more successful than you" – or help you avoid the landmines that you have observed so you don't figuratively blow yourself up.

While contemplating what I wanted to say, I went to a thesaurus only to discover some fabulous synonyms for the word observation. It said, surveillance, scrutiny, watching, inspection, examination, and study. These are all great words in and of themselves – and all characteristics of success.

By the way, I think you will find it interesting to know that the antonym for observation is *neglect*, which means to abandon, avoid, disregard, and overlook.

I am asking you to be aware, to notice things, to see what works and what doesn't, to have "non-experience experiences" that guide you on a surer pathway to your goals. Let me explain. You can put your hand in a fire and have a first hand experience of being burned – or you can witness another put their hand in a fire, hear them scream with pain and smell the flesh burning. That is a non-experience experience because you learned not to put your hand in the fire without having to hurt yourself. Likewise, you can do that on the positive side. Observe successful people, watch the way they walk, the speed and certainty of the way they talk, the manner in which they dress for all occasions. Watch their body language, their facial expressions, and how they use their hands to communicate. Look closely at their offices, notice the organization and neatness, their team, their confidence, the way they handle adversity and the policies and procedures that seem to work successfully.

Then, all you have to do is add your unique and special personality and sit back and watch the Law of Attraction do its magic. You will be impressed with the Power of Observation.

THE "A" TEAM

One of the most overlooked, yet ultra-important ingredients for success is for any entrepreneur to surround him or herself with the "right" people, especially the ones you work with everyday – your employees. Do not underestimate the value of not only interviewing and selecting the one whom you feel is the best person for every available position in your business, but also having the desire and know-how to shape them into your "A" Team.

It is simply not good enough to hire a "nice" person, one who shows up every day, does his or her job fairly well, goes home and starts all over again the next day. Rather, the idea is to hire right, terminate quickly if a mistake has been made, and spend an extraordinary amount of time in two areas – training and accountability.

Training does not mean that a senior employee haphazardly trains a new employee and the owner is devoid of responsibilities. It means that the boss, leader or entrepreneur takes a large part in the training, having a training, training and training again philosophy which is the cornerstone of creating a fully-engaged, turned-on knowledgeable and caring employee, one who is desirous of being part of a team that believes in the leadership and in the purpose and mission statement of that company.

The "boss" trains the employee on the intangible aspects of the business, such as its purpose, mission and vision and what it is that he or she actually expects from his team. This is to insure that all employees have clarity as to what is expected from them and what you can, in turn, expect from their performance.

The owner/leader should also play a huge part in interactive training and actually should have regular rehearsals pertaining to office concepts and policies as well as the phrases and sentences used by all members of the team.

Also under the heading of training, the employee should be given some "homework" responsibilities that will help provide deeper understanding and additional knowledge. Perhaps they are asked to read and report back on a chapter in a book or an article or listen to a CD. Maybe they have to do some online study or join a mastermind alliance.

What matters is that training is viewed as a never-ending process, and I will even be bold enough to state that, in my opinion, it takes two full years to thoroughly train an employee and turn them into a true paraprofessional, regardless of occupation or kind of business.

Second to training comes accountability, an easily understood word, but an area that is weak in almost every business I have studied. Being accountable comes from being sufficiently trained so you feel confident and then openly reporting what you have accomplished so that the owner and fellow employees can be kept abreast of what progress you are making in completing your assigned tasks.

I know a CEO who is particularly adroit in holding his "A" Team accountable. At the end of each week every one of them is required to shoot him an email telling him what they have accomplished that week, how their department is doing, what needs to be accomplished and any ideas that can contribute to making things better. He then not only knows what is going on at all times but uses this information to report back to the entire team during team meetings. These emails are then collected and used during periodic employee reviews.

This is breakthrough technology and it is not difficult to implement. An added benefit is that if someone is out for any reason or if they are terminated or decide to quit, you know where you stand and what you need to do to stay up to speed.

Training and accountability are key ingredients that all leaders utilize to build their "A" Team, avoid the staleness of rogue repetition, and engage everyone in the process of constant improvement.

There should never be a time when the boss (and anyone on the team) is not improving himself personally, professionally, or technologically. Plateaus or stagnant businesses come from doing the same old thing over and over again because people are either under-trained or not held accountable or are afraid to make changes.

Clean up these two areas and most assuredly your business will run more smoothly and efficiently. The only caveat, of course, is that the owner must exhibit the characteristics of leadership: be strong, decisive and organized, so that the staff respects the leader and is willing to act accordingly.

Lastly, when you think all of the above is accomplished – take a deep breath and train again!

UNCOVERING TIMELY PRINCIPLES

After years of mentoring and coaching others, I have discovered a simple truth that, while often overlooked, is to me an imperative key to all long-lasting success.

It is with absolute certainty that I can state that those who have managed to build the biggest businesses and the best personal lives are those who have laid a solid foundation upon which they have built their buildings. That is precisely why they seem to stay on top of the heap, year after year, and when adversity does strike or they falter in any way, they always seem to bounce back and move even farther forward.

They appear to the entire world to be visionaries, when the fact is that everything that they ARE, DO, and HAVE is based upon the core ideologies and timeless principles they established at the onset.

Core ideologies are basic precepts that say, "This is who I am -- this is what I stand for -- this is what I am all about." These are not just idle words, they are *vital shaping forces* -- I repeat, *vital shaping forces*!

My businesses always have core values and to a large extent that is why we have been able to create our success. Core values are an organization's essential and enduring tenets, their set of guiding principles, and the inherent values that can never be compromised for financial gain or expediency.

We believe in heroic customer, client, or patient service, being on the leading edge and that good enough is not good enough. We believe that people, especially the people we serve, are the *source of our strength;* that basic honesty and integrity are not only the best way, but the only way.

We believe in the immutable Law of Cause and Effect – that success comes *from* you, not *to* you; that winners have a passion to serve that far exceeds their compulsion to survive.

We believe that we exist to help as many people as possible turn on *their* Prosperity Faucets. We believe in continuity and stability, but urge continued and constant, never-ending change.

It is with certainty that we have come to know without a shadow of a doubt that "It's All In Your Head," that success or prosperity cannot flow into clutter, that our Mothers, Fathers, Teachers and Preachers (MFTPs) have had an extraordinary role in shaping our self-images, that if you are not early, you are late, and that in this world you should have a rule that your fee, is your fee, is your fee.

And, to me at least, the grand-daddy of all laws is Circle-Circle (if your intents and actions are truthful, your experience will match your intents), your intents and actions must be congruent. Further, that The Law of Cause and Effect is as absolute and dependable as the sun rising in the east and setting in the west.

We ask you to have the courage of your convictions, to suck-it-up and bite-the-bullet and have the courage to travel through your own passage of pain, the one that will lead you to the proverbial pot of gold found at the end of a magnificent and brilliant seven-color rainbow.

FACING UP

S omeone once said that if you were interested in finding the cause of all your mistakes and failures, look in a mirror. While at first that expression might be dismissed as just trivial nonsense, at second glance, it really has some merit.

Because your concepts, thinking, understanding, emotional pre-programming, memory, courage or fear formed part of every action you make, all mistakes and failures that you experience have a lot to do with the person looking back at you in that mirror. This doesn't mean that you are bad or dumb or not wanting to succeed; it just indicates that either you just didn't know enough, did not have the right information or thought that the action steps you took in and of themselves were enough.

It really doesn't matter! What matters is not how you ACT, only how you REACT to any mistake, error, failure or setback that comes your way. What matters is that you face up and learn from what didn't go right, face up to the failure without using self-defeating emotion or behavior. Instead, carefully examine the whole issue and make a list of the lessons learned and the distinctions made in the process.

Facing up means discovering the internal truth about who you are, and then ameliorating those thoughts or actions with new foresight, courage and action. And I caution you, that "trying" to succeed by doing the same old thing, by repeating the thoughts, plans or actions of something that failed, will *never* bring about desired results – *never!*

Worse yet is recognizing the weakness and believing that just because you have discovered the problem, it will go away by talking about it or telling yourself what you *have to do.* For instance, who says, "I have to quit smoking"? Smokers say that! Who says, "I just have to stop drinking"? Alcoholics say that! And who says (verbally or non-verbally) "I am not confrontational enough" or "I am afraid"? People who are non-confrontational and those who are in fear of a negative consequence, of course.

Knowing who you are and attempting to take more actions will not necessarily bring about better results. Nor will doing daily affirmations or half-time locker-room pep-talks from a well meaning coach. "You can do it, go for it, give it all you've got," or "Have courage, be determined, focus in, energize and keep your eye on the ball." All good stuff, but simply not enough because the root cause of the failures or mistakes has not been handled.

In order to change the results you are getting, *you must first change your belief system.* If internally you fear rejection, you will automatically be less confrontational and the words you select or the actions you take will be laced with the seeds of failure because you will lack certainty, authority, and authenticity. The key is Facing Up to the fact that if your beliefs create your reality, all you have to do to change the results you get is to purposely and deliberately *change your mind* and *alter your belief system.*

Amazingly enough, this does not take days, weeks, or years. It only takes a few minutes. You can decide to have courage instead of fear. You can decide to tell customers what they truly need and not what you think they will accept. You can decide that building a better business is now a priority to you and you can let go of the rationalizations, excuses and defense mechanisms you have used over and over again to no avail.

Instead of saying, "I want to get more new business" and fooling yourself into thinking that direct mailings or passive advertising will do, what would happen if you changed your belief system to include the fact that people in general are just interested in what you have to say? I'll bet it would have a dramatically positive effect on the results you get. Face Up – change your beliefs and your new beliefs will change the emotions and actions you put out, and what goes around, does come around.

THE STORY OF
WILLIE COOLIE

Thirty years ago, when I was first experiencing my own personal growth and practice success, I was invited to be the speaker at the Tennessee Chiropractic Association's Annual Convention held that year in Memphis. It was a time in my career when I was taking seminars by the dozen, devouring self-help books, listening to motivational tapes and meeting with any person whose life or business was more successful than my own. And, since that was everyone, I was one busy man. I was, after all, hot on the trail of and in active pursuit of success!

After collecting my baggage from the carousel, I proceeded outside to find a taxi that would take me to the hotel. To my surprise, there was no taxi line and, in fact, no taxis were in sight. Obviously, the dispatcher noticed the look on my face because he instantly blew a whistle to hail a cab from the bullpen, where taxis park and wait for fares.

So there I was, all dressed up (that's how people flew in those days) with new luggage, waiting for the taxi to arrive. When it finally pulled up in front of me, I was kind of flabbergasted and didn't quite know what to do. Trust me when I say that my ego told me to run. After all, why should, you'll excuse the expression, "a success like me" have to ride in a banged-up cab with scratches and dents all over it? My studies were all urging me to go "first class" and this taxi was not even close.

I was debating what to do when the driver jumped from the cab, seemed to vault over the hood and run around the car, looking me straight in the eye and with a great big smile said, "Hi, I'm Willie Coolie. Welcome to Tennessee." Then, before I could recover, he lifted my luggage, very carefully and gently and placed the bags side by side on the floor of the trunk. He closed the lid, making sure it was secure and ran around to the right rear passenger door of the cab, opened it, stood to one side, bowed ever so slightly, pointed to the back seat and said, "Please watch your head and be careful stepping in."

What would you do?

Yeah, me too! I got in, and was immediately surprised to find that the inside of the cab was so immaculate - and I mean immaculate! It smelled clean and fresh, there were new seat covers and floor mats, the windows were clean, the ash trays were washed out and even those little signs that adorn every cab in America were put up straight - and in frames! I'll admit that the New Yorker in me was starting to be just a little skeptical. Something began to nag at me and the hairs on the back of my neck were beginning to stand up.

Willie, once again, ran around the car, this time to the driver's side and got in, being careful not to slam the door. He buckled up, pulled out, drove until he was out of the way of airport traffic and then pulled over to the side, stopped the car, turned around to face me, and with a big grin said, "Dr. Markson, may I ask you a few questions?"

When, with a frown of continued skepticism, I responded affirmatively, he continued by asking me if this was my first visit to Memphis, my destination, my occupation, how many children I had, and finally, was my trip for business purposes or for relaxation and pleasure?

There went those hairs again, this time with warning bells! I felt as if I were on a witness stand, not in a cab trying to get to a hotel. My mind became more alert, and I answered carefully, saying that this was indeed my first time in Tennessee, that I was going to the Hyatt Hotel, and that I was a chiropractor, had a daughter named Danna and a son named Rick, and I was invited as a guest speaker of the Tennessee Chiropractic Association.

He then smiled at me and told me to sit back and get comfortable, because he knew exactly where the Hyatt was, that it was a great hotel worth the few extra minutes of travel time and that he would get me there safely in about 30 minutes, give or take traffic conditions. The taxi eased away from the curb and before I knew it we were cruising along.

Recap 1

The poor first impression, because of the beat-up outside appearance of the cab was quickly reversed by Willie's energy, enthusiasm and careful attention to detail – direct eye contact, smile and greeting, the way he handled my luggage and invited me to step into the cab, the fact that he didn't slam his door and even called me by name. How did he know my name anyway? I surely didn't tell him. That's correct! He was observant and read my name off the luggage tags. Then, he asked me some opening questions, sizing me up as I responded and whether he had a "spectator" or a "participator" as a customer. I wouldn't doubt that he was doing a personality profile at the same time.

Then he let me know that he was an experienced driver, had prior knowledge of the hotel, and knew the best route and the time it took to get there. What else was left but to sit back and let this journey unfold?

When we were driving for a few minutes, Willie asked me if I preferred to ride in silence or, since this was my first trip to Memphis, would I prefer to hear a little bit about local points of interest. Well, I thought, in for a dime, in for a dollar.

The next thing I knew, he reached down on the front seat and handed me a zippered leather portfolio, which he asked me to open to page one. As I did so, he asked me if I could read a map. When I told him I could, he enthusiastically said, "Good!" and told me to place my left index finger on the big star on the bottom left hand corner (the airport) and then with my right index finger find coordinates F4 on the upper right part of the map. When I did, Willie told me that he liked his customers to "know where they were and where they were going."

For the next few minutes, he told me some interesting facts and colorful stories about Memphis. Further, he told me that he would be driving right past the site of the proposed new Tennessee Chiropractic Association Headquarters building, now under construction, a fact gleaned from the local newspaper, I came to find out. This guy was incredible!

Graceland

I then, at his request, turned the page of the portfolio and found myself staring incredulously, at a fancy pink mansion. When I became silent, Willie asked if I knew what I was looking at. I grunted no, he exclaimed as if everyone in the world should have known, "Why, Dr. Markson, that's Graceland – Elvis Presley's home!"

Willie said, "You know, Doc, if you have just a few extra minutes, I could whiz you by Graceland. After all, how can you come all this way without visiting Graceland? What would you tell Danna and Rick?" My first feeling was one of cynicism. Did Willie set me up just to take me to Graceland and get the extra fare? I suppose he also had a cousin who was waiting there to sell me some souvenirs! It didn't matter anymore because his charm was so infectious that I put my suspicions on hold. I simply told him that I preferred to go directly to the hotel, and that, for now, we would skip Graceland.

When we pulled up under the portico of the Hyatt Hotel, Willie opened the trunk from the button inside the glove compartment and leapt out of the cab, catching the lid before it started to vibrate when it reached the fully open position. He lifted my bags from the trunk, placed them side by side on the pavement near the rear door of the cab, and almost without losing stride, opened the door for me. I got out of the cab, not knowing quite what to feel, but somehow I "knew" that I was witnessing perfection in customer service.

Your "customers" will get the same feeling, if they are indeed receiving the special service you always say you provide. That experience was reinforced when Willie called the doorman over and said, "Albert, this is Dr. Markson, a VIP who is in from New York to speak to the Tennessee Chiropractic Association. This is also his first time in Tennessee, so treat him with the good old Southern hospitality that will make him come back again." Truthfully, I was starting to pay attention to whatever Willie said or did.

There was only one more piece of business to be taken care of, so in the traditional manner, I asked Willie how much I owed him. He looked through the window at the meter and said, "That will be twenty-one dollars, Dr. Markson" (remember, this was thirty years ago), "and I hope you enjoyed the ride." I fished through my money clip and realized that the smallest bills I had with me were twenties. Not convenient, but not a big problem. I took out two twenties and handed them over.

It was then that I experienced the greatest monetary confrontation in the history of my thirty-five-year business career. Nothing again has even come close to the perfected style of Willie Coolie! Willie took the money, snapped the bills like a bank teller, looked at the cash in his hand, took a giant step closer to me, put on the biggest smile I had ever seen, focused his eyes directly into mine as if they were laser beams and said with a voice so confident that it is hard to describe, "Dr. Markson, how much do you want back, less my tip, of course?"

I tell you, it was brilliant! The message was delivered in such a way that it was impossible to think him impudent or rude. He knew exactly what his service was worth and he had absolutely no trouble asking for commensurate compensation. This is hot stuff!

Again, what would you do? Yeah, me too! All thoughts of my customary paltry tipping habits were instantly abandoned and I heard myself saying, "Just give me back ten dollars, Willie. You deserve a little extra for the terrific service." A nine-dollar gratuity! That's a forty-three percent tip!

I said goodbye and turned to go into the hotel to register. But, as I did so, Willie asked if he was permitted one more question. I said, "Sure, Willie, go ahead. I don't think I could stop you if I wanted to." He countered with, "Dr. Markson, I have learned that when I drive someone *from* the airport, they usually need a ride *back* to the airport when they depart. Would it okay with you if I was waiting right here to pick you up to whisk you back to the airport when you came out of the hotel?" Well, what would you say this time? Yeah, me too!

In the flash of any eye, Willie leaned through the open right front window of the cab and lifted out an appointment book, which he promptly opened, while asking for the date of my departure. I told him it was the next day, and he asked, "What time is your plane leaving and when you go to an airport, Dr. Markson, how much cushion do you like to build in, so you feel comfortable that you won't be late?" I told him that my plane was scheduled to leave at 3:00 P.M. and that I like to be at the airport a minimum of one hour or so before departure. He made some mental calculations and said, "How would it work for you, if was here waiting at about 12:45 p.m. In my book, if you are not early, you are late! You never know what to expect with Sunday traffic."

Willie then handed me a beautifully designed and printed business card on one side and appointment card on the other on which he had written, "Sunday, 12:45 p.m. – Markson to airport." And, he said, "You know, doc, I make my living driving a cab and, on occasion, important people like you get so busy that your plans can change on the spot. If that happens, would you please be respectful enough to call me so I can replace the lost time with another customer who could use my services? *Repeat business is the name of the game for all people who want to be successful.*" Incredulous, I shook my head in amazement, said goodbye, and headed into the hotel to register and get on with the purpose of my trip.

Recap 2

My time in Willie's office was used for educational and informational purposes. Remember the portfolio with the map, photos of Graceland and points of interest, including the construction site of the new Tennessee Chiropractic Association building? You see, Willie had a great self-image and a large vision. He saw himself as being in the travel business, not merely a taxi driver.

He tried to sell me the side trip to Graceland, but when I objected, he didn't push the issue and just let it go so as not to make me uncomfortable.

Control was re-established by his great attitude and superior service when we arrived at the hotel. Cleverly, Willie added forty-three percent to his fare because he had developed incredible people skills. He believed in himself and believed that you serve and then you receive.

Lastly, he doubled his business and doubled his income by making another appointment for the return trip.

The next day, having delivered what I considered to be an excellent talk, I gathered my belongings, checked out of the hotel, and headed for the front entrance, preparing to depart for the airport.

When I got outside, I glanced around looking for Willie's cab, which was hard to miss. To my amazement, there was no sign of him. A glance at my watch told me that it was only 12:30 p.m. I was early, so I decided to sit down and wait.

As I was searching for a place to sit, I spotted Willie's cab parked on the side, in the shade about 50 feet to the right of the portico. I walked over to tell Willie that I was ready, but as I approached I noticed that he was not there. Figuring that I was early and maybe he went for a bite to eat, I turned to walk back. Just as I did, out of the corner of my eye, I saw that the left rear door of the cab was ajar. I walked around the taxi, thinking I would close it and to my astonishment, I saw two legs sticking out. My curiosity was peaked and I walked up to the open door, looked in and found Willie Coolie with a rag in one hand and a spray bottle in the other. He was cleaning the car and washing the ashtrays.

I cleared my throat to get his attention and Willie jumped out of the car, gave me the million-dollar smile and said, "Hi, Dr. Markson, it's great to see you again. How did your lectures go?" "Terrific," I exclaimed as I watched him run over to my luggage, pick up the two pieces, run back to the cab, open the trunk and place them gently inside. No surprise this time because I had become accustomed to the great service and subconsciously came to expect it.

He continued, "Dr. Markson, before we pull away, I want you to be sure you didn't forget something." I reflected for a moment and told him I was sure I had taken everything with me, but asked what made him think I had forgotten something. His reply showed the keen sense of observation always utilized by those who enjoy success. Willie said, with eyebrows of concern, "I just couldn't help noticing that your luggage was lighter today than it was yesterday." Now it was my time to smile, almost laugh in fact, as I offered the explanation that I was fortunate enough to sell some of my albums to a very appreciative audience.

"That's great," said Willie, as he ran around to the passenger door and repeated the same initial "enter the cab procedure" he had used the day before. Only this time, when we drove far enough away from the hotel to be out of harm's way, he pulled over and turned around to offer me the following proposition.

Can you figure out what it was?

Come on, I've been doing all the talking. Can you guess what Willie was going to say or what his agile little mind was planning? I'll admit I was a bit nonplussed, until the plot began to unveil itself. Willie, with his customary smile and magnetic charm, asked me if he was right in recalling that yesterday I had told him I was most comfortable arriving at an airport about one hour prior to departure.

He then nodded his head with self-satisfaction and blurted out, "Dr. Markson, this is terrific because now you don't have to disappoint Danna and Rick. It is two hours and 25 minutes until your departure and we have plenty of time to swing by Graceland and pick up a memento or two for the kids. What do you say, yes?" He used that facial expression and that laser beam stare again…and he became totally silent, awaiting my answer.

Graceland was wonderful.

Don't be so proud of yourself. I think you would have gone too.... and it was indeed exciting to be there. I had a fabulous tour and bought out the store – gifts for everyone who was an Elvis enthusiast.

So, what do you think? Were the tour guides and gift shop operators Willie's cousins? The answer, of course, was no, and I knew that! Anyone with Willie's kind of success consciousness and service orientation was surely a person who was in possession of integrity and high ethics.

At long last, we pulled up in front of the airport. It was exactly 1:45 p.m., sixty minutes prior to departure (you had no doubt, did you?), and we repeated the arrival ritual. Eventually we got to the time when I had to ask, "How much do I owe you, Willie?" I could hardly wait to hear the number, especially in light of the side trip to Graceland and the waiting time while I browsed.

Willie immediately responded by saying, "That will be twenty-one dollars, Doc!" Smiling, I said in return, "Willie, you've forgotten about Graceland."

"No, I didn't," he passionately blurted out. "The Graceland trip is on me. I just couldn't let you visit Tennessee and not go there. It was worth seeing your face, and it was my pleasure."

Arguing didn't help, so I finally took out two twenties again and handed them over. Willie took them from me, snapped them like a bank teller does, took a giant step forward, flashed those brilliant teeth, honed in on my pupils and said, "Dr. Markson, how much do you want back, less my tip, of course?"

Well, come on, spit it out. What would you do? Yeah, me too! The words were tumbling out of my mouth before I had a chance to think, "Willie, it's all yours!" He thanked me graciously, but I suspected he got exactly what he expected! In case you are interested, that's a ninety percent tip!

Before escaping to the safety of the airport, I had to ask one or two questions of my own. "Willie," I said, "if it's not too presumptuous of me, may I ask how you do – financially, that is?" He looked both ways, making sure he wasn't overheard and said, "Actually, quite well, thank you. My business is booming, my children are in good schools, we've bought a nice little house, and from my ten percent savings account, I purchased an ice cream franchise that is run by my wife. The extra income goes toward savings and into college funds for the kids." Continuing, he said, "And to think, Doc, that eighty percent of the cabbies I know are struggling. They spend their time complaining about the customers, the starters, their bosses, the price of auto insurance, and the cost of gas. I'm a fortunate man because I don't have time for all that. My spare time is used to invent ways to deliver better service."

"Last question Willie. Something has been bothering me from the beginning and I'm dying to know why your taxi is so beat up in appearance. It doesn't fit because everything else you do is so first class. You are a walking, talking, living example of excellence and the beat-up cab is so incongruent – it doesn't make any sense to me."

Willie smiled and said, "Dr. Markson, I learned a long time ago to *concentrate on the things I can control and pay no attention to things out of my control.* You see, the owner of the cab doesn't want to spend the money to repair my taxi. I'm sure that eventually he will, but until that time, I focus on the things I can control, like the inside of the cab, my attitude and the service I deliver."

Willie then glanced down at his watch and told me he had to run because he had more business waiting. He hopped in the cab while telling me not to forget to call him if I ever got the opportunity to return to Memphis. As he drove away, I realized I was standing in front of the airport, following the cab as it made its way toward the exit. I was in awe, shaking my head in amazement and I'm certain that my mouth was wide open.

The Story of Willie Coolie, Cab Driver Extraordinaire!

This metaphorical story is intended as a method of sharing with you some of the lessons learned from this most unusual experience. What attitudes, actions, or procedures can you think of to use in your life and, more importantly, what do you think the end results would be? Yeah, me too!

Talking To Yourself Is Not Crazy

Who We Are and What We Do

ABOUT DR. LARRY MARKSON

Dr. Larry Markson, Personal Empowerment, Practice & Business Success and Prosperity Coach to countless thousands of people has devoted his professional life to helping others transform their thoughts, actions and feelings until they are able to experience the fulfillment of their life's goals.

For the first 19 years of his career, Larry was a practicing Doctor of Chiropractic who owned a high volume, extremely successful, multi-doctor practice – the Queens Chiropractic Center in Flushing, New York.

In 1980, after a career-ending injury, he founded Markson Management Services, a strategy-based practice management and coaching firm for Chiropractors. MMS gained national recognition for the results they achieved in helping thousands of DCs build better practices.

In 1997, after transforming his thinking to the ideologies expressed in this book, he co-founded The Masters Circle, an identity-based personal coaching and seminar company that taught chiropractors and their key assistants how to expand their concepts and visions in addition to their professional expertise.

In 2006, Dr. Markson founded what he considers to be his best, certainly his favorite, venture. It is called The Cabin Experience

– a Breaking Free - Personal Freedom Retreat for twenty-five people at a time. His website, www.thecabinexperience.com, contains the details of The Cabin, as it is affectionately called.

Larry believes that your business, practice, and/or your personal life are waiting for a leader (YOU) to show up and that it is who you are and not only what you do that determines the results you will experience in life.

Now, in his fifth decade of sharing the secrets of success with audiences from 50 to 8,000 worldwide, he is an in-demand keynote or platform speaker who believes that it is successful people who build successful businesses and lives – and that "Success comes FROM you, not TO you!"

Dr. Larry Markson's

"THE CABIN EXPERIENCE"

A Breaking Free - Personal Freedom Retreat

The Cabin Experience is a 2½ day Breaking Free - Personal Freedom Retreat held in a log cabin hotel, located right in the middle of fantastically beautiful Salmon Lake, Montana.

Breaking Free from whom, you might ask? Breaking Free from YOU is the answer. Breaking Free from all the STUFF that has clouded your brain and made you put your foot on the brakes to achievement, all the STUFF that has held you back from being or doing anything you wanted to BE or DO, so you could HAVE what you really want.

The Personal Freedom acquired at The Cabin Experience will enable you to gain courage, make instant decisions and fulfill more of YOUR dreams – and do all of it without guilt, anger, blame, worry or fear! Never again will another person or past event rule over who you are and what you can do.

The Cabin Experience is an intense and amazing, totally interactive 60-hour personal growth conclave, designed to get you in touch with your inner self while showing you how to successfully deal with your past, handle the present and invent a future that works for your benefit – deliberately and on purpose.

The Cabin Experience is not just another seminar with some self-proclaimed wizard standing there teaching and telling you what to DO. On the contrary, TCE is a totally interactive process by which you come to discover and realize exactly who you are and what your real potential is – by yourself! That's why it works!

The Cabin Experience is about creating abundant health, wonderful relationships, a thriving business, and financial freedom. And, how would you like to be able to shed all negatives and hurts from your past, override past remorse, turn fear to faith and transform your energy field so you can actually attract into your life whatever it is you want?

Perhaps a better question is, "How would you react if you had the opportunity to pick my brain, share my experience of success and happiness and receive my personal attention for 2½ days?"

What makes The Cabin Experience so unique and special is that it affords you the opportunity to work with terrific people who are, like you, serious about success and personal fulfillment. Those who have attended previous Cabin events have told me that this experience helped them open up and provided them with the tools that would allow them to approach their futures with certainty and confidence. Wow! How exciting is that?

This much I can promise you. If you are willing to lock yourself up with me for 2½ days with no distractions, no formalities, no cell phones, no computers and a very casual dress code – and if you come with high expectations, you will walk out an entirely different person than the one who walked in. In fact, I guarantee that you have never had an experience of this kind before.

A PERSONAL NOTE FROM ME

You will find that The Cabin Experience is not about me teaching you anything, or you learning something didactic that will save your life or improve it. This experience is about insight and how you can use the insight gained here to move you along on your journey toward Happiness, Fulfillment, and Freedom, which is what we all want in the first place.

The Cabin Experience is about putting you in a place where you are uncomfortable, a place where you cannot run and hide, because unless you do that you *cannot* grow. This is about you facing and fixing some of your weaker areas – because you can only grow as much as your weaker areas allow.

It is also about putting before you, into your consciousness, for your eventual digestion and use, the POSSIBILITIES that are open to you in the future.

Possibilities are just opportunities waiting for your imagination to grab, sketch and your emotions to agree with.

Remember, creative and successful people live in their imaginations – their dream rooms.

While at The Cabin Experience, we will get to know each other intimately and we will come to admire and know each other's strengths and weaknesses as well. We will create a safe, judgment-free environment – one in which you can explore who you are and not be hurt, intimidated, embarrassed or mortally wounded.

At The Cabin I will ask you to let your defenses down, learn to trust the process and know that whatever happens, you WILL survive and grow from the experience.

Personal growth is serious stuff and I ask you to respect that – what you think is easy, someone else feels is paralyzing; what you feel comfortable doing, someone else struggles with – and if I wanted to I could expose everyone – but, that is not why people choose to come.

The 2½ days spent at The Cabin Experience are about Breaking Free and Personal Freedom! Freedom to soar, to attract what you want, freedom to fall in love, make changes with ease and freedom to get rich mentally, emotionally and financially.

I want you to know RIGHT NOW that most of the problems you have ever experienced or are now experiencing *do not belong to you*! They belonged to others and *you got attached to them.* By the end of The Cabin Experience I fully expect you to remove the badge of honor that comes with illness (mentally, like fear or poverty, or physically, being sick so you can't be expected to perform) or misfortune of any kind. I want you to be clear on the fact that when you leave TCE you will be able to RESOLVE the REASONS for Unhappiness, Failure, Sickness, Poverty, and Uncertainty. And, you will have all the resources you need to overcome them.

Does that sound good to you? A better question is, "Are you WILLING to RISK so you can discover the true dimensions of your unlimited potential or are you here because you think it is the right thing to do to fool yourself into believing you are serious about changing, about shedding, about growing?"

I want you to remember that inner success is never a matter of adding anything – *it is purely a shedding process.* You were born to be successful, healthy, and happy and you took or added ingredients and habits that block the actions designed to help you achieve success. This event is about shedding and awakening in a new light.

TCE is not full of negatives that will depress you, nor is it a pep rally meant to artificially and temporarily build you up and make you feel better so you feel you got your money's worth. Instead it is about making the discoveries, the distinctions and acknowledgements that will allow you to change course in the middle of your life – allow you to reach higher, up toward light, and allow you to achieve your heart's desire.

Are you ready to begin and trust the process? Are you committed – totally committed and passionate about building a new you? If the answer is yes, then The Cabin Experience is for you!

AN OPEN INVITATION

You are cordially invited to go online and check out our website, www.thecabinexperience.com and subscribe to our Article of the Week. While you are at it, why not consider calling me personally to determine if The Cabin Experience is a good fit for you?

Larry's Contact Information:

Dr. Larry Markson
LTM Consulting, Inc.
2565 NW 59th Street
Boca Raton, FL 33496

Office phone: 561 995-0946
Cell phone: 516 318-1444
larry@ltmconsulting.net
www.thecabinexperience.com

CPSIA information can be obtained at www.ICGtesting.com
Printed in the USA
LVOW05s0222071114

412410LV00002B/2/P